The Art
of Paper
Flowers

Quarto is the authority on a wide range of topics.
Quarto educates, entertains and enriches the lives of
our readers—enthusiasts and lovers of hands-on living.
www.QuartoKnows.com

First published in the United States
of America in 2016 by Rockport Publishers,
an Imprint of Quarto Publishing Group USA Inc.
100 Cummings Center / Suite 406-L
Beverly, Massachusetts 01915-6101
Telephone: (978) 282-9590
Fax: (978) 283-2742
QuartoKnows.com
Visit our blogs at QuartoKnows.com

10 9 8 7 6 5 4 3 2 1

ISBN: 978-1-58923-936-4

eISBN: 978-1-63159-158-7

Library of Congress
Cataloging-in-Publication
Data available.

Design
Timothy Samara

Photography
**Scott Peterson
Productions, Inc.**

Printed in China

The Art of Paper Flowers

Bobby Pearce

Creating Realistic Blossoms from Ordinary Papers

FOREWORD BY
Rosie O'Donnell

Creative Publishing international

Contents

The Basics

The Flowers

ACKNOWLEDGMENTS

Janette Barber
Ruby Link
Rosie O'Donnell
Doug Turshen
Anne Re
Scott Peterson
Leo Daignault
Ken Gray
Kathy Sheldon
Leigh Kamioner
Elizabeth Evans
Laura Biagi
Linda Neubauer
John Gettings

DEDICATION

To Grandma Ruby, who started it all—
and her daughter, Barbara (my mom),
whose love and encouragement
made me the person I am today.

Foreword

I love this book. Not because my friend Bobby—or as I like to call him Tony-Nominated Costume Designer Bobby Pearce—wrote it, but because it's exquisite and beautiful. And it's coming out at a time when we, as a society, can best soothe our troubled souls with calmer minds. In other words: let's get crafting. Crafting, for me, is moving meditation—a chance to immerse myself in color and form with such absorption that the metaphorical dragons and demons go back to their caves and sit in silence while I release my soul through the creativity of my hands. Oh yes. Crafting is much more than colored paper.

I've known Bobby forever. Our shared passion for crafting is part of the fabric of our friendship. You can give Bobby a hanger and a piece of tissue paper and he could make a chandelier. I've seen it. He has worked as my craft expert on all of my shows. I don't think anyone who has seen it will ever forget Bobby singing dressed as Queen Elizabeth—a costume that I'm pretty sure he deftly created out of gum and Red Hots! He was the secret sauce that made my own craft book the success that it was. This guy has the chops, and he knows how to communicate his skills. He's done it with me for decades.

I don't know what I love most in this book. The book itself is a piece of art. Every single flower in it was designed and created by Bobby, personally, so that he could be sure that anyone could follow his patterns. Bobby is a perfectionist. I like that. He has created perfection in an imperfect world. It's exactly what I was in the mood for after watching the news this morning! I'm happy that you will get to know my friend Bobby through the stories he shares in this book. Listen, I know the guy . . . it might seem like no one could be this wonderfully quirky, but—surprise—here's Bobby! He's the real deal, and so is *The Art of Paper Flowers*. Enjoy it in as many ways as you like: for the beauty in its pages, the humor and heart in its words, or the patterns and instructions that will let you create crafts as beautiful as Bobby's. Me, I'm going for all three.

ROSIE O'DONNELL

Introduction

I remember many a rainy South Florida day, sitting at Grandma Ruby's kitchen table making flowers. My grandmother was very proud of her floral creations. From a foot or two away, you honestly couldn't tell one of Grandma's flowers from the real thing in her garden. The secret to Grandma's lifelike petals was a product called "wood fibre."

Wood fibre was made from the pith of *Aralia papyrifera*, a species of bamboo that grew in the swamps on the Island of Formosa in the China Sea. Sheets of the plant's pith, resembling a moist rice paper, were dyed beautiful colors. From the 1950s though the '70s, you could easily find wood fibre in craft stores; unfortunately, it is not manufactured today.

After Grandma passed away, her wood fibre crafts were packed up and set aside for me. Some forty years later, I found myself sitting at my own kitchen table, staring into the crate of Grandma's wood fibre flower supplies. Wire, floral tape, artificial leaves, stamens, Grandma's treasured flower patterns, and even rare blocks of unopened wood fibre were staring back at me. I was eight years old again.

Grandma's flower patterns were a labor of love. She would work for hours on the details, often pulling apart real flowers to check the petals against her own renditions. Once she was happy with her patterns, my grandfather (who had owned a roofing company) would cut the shapes out of tin sheets so his wife's patterns would last forever.

I decided not to open or use the rare and precious wood fibre; instead, I chose to craft Grandma's flowers using colorful scrapbooking, craft, and construction papers. Ironic if you think about it: paper was once a plant, and I am using paper to craft a plant once again.

This book contains Grandma's original patterns (which I have adapted to be used with paper) and my complete instructions for each flower. I hope bringing these flowers to life gives you as much joy and as many memories as this craft has given me.

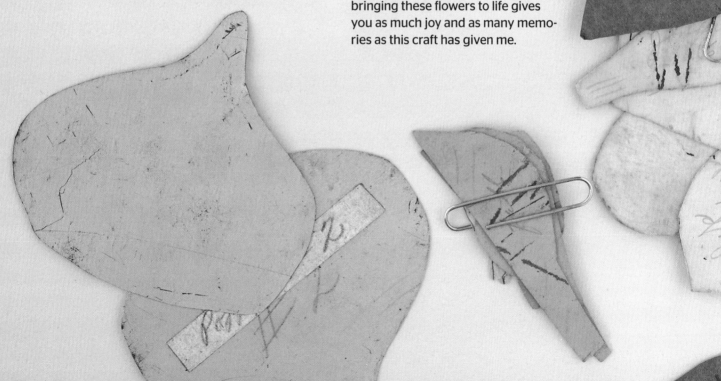

The Basics

Before I begin any craft I like to make sure I have everything I need right in front of me. There is nothing more frustrating than getting to a certain point in a project only to discover that you are missing a tool or material needed to complete what you started!

Petal
The colorful part of the flower.

Calyx
The calyx is made up of sepals, which look like tiny green leaves. It covers and protects the bud before the flower opens.

Stem
The main body or stalk supporting the flower.

Pistil
This is the female part of the flower. It's the sticky part in the center of the flower that catches pollen grains.

Stamen
The male part of the flower. This is where the pollen is produced.

Petiole
The stalk attaching a leaf to a stem.

Blade
The broad part of a leaf.

Veins
Strands of vascular tissue forming the framework of the leaf.

PARTS OF THE FLOWER

It is not necessary to have a scientific knowledge of a flower's anatomy to create these paper flowers. However, it is helpful to be familiar with some of the basic terms used in this book.

Materials

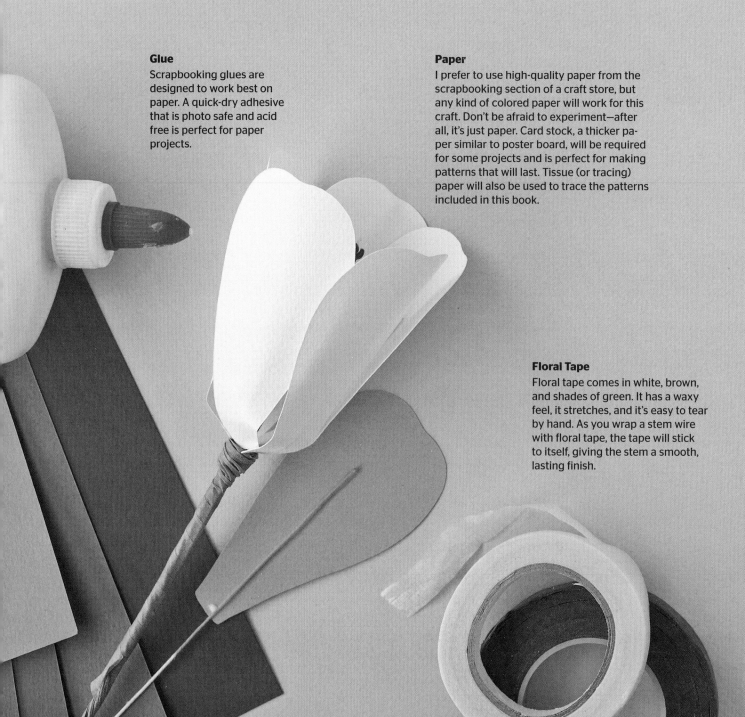

Glue

Scrapbooking glues are designed to work best on paper. A quick-dry adhesive that is photo safe and acid free is perfect for paper projects.

Paper

I prefer to use high-quality paper from the scrapbooking section of a craft store, but any kind of colored paper will work for this craft. Don't be afraid to experiment—after all, it's just paper. Card stock, a thicker paper similar to poster board, will be required for some projects and is perfect for making patterns that will last. Tissue (or tracing) paper will also be used to trace the patterns included in this book.

Floral Tape

Floral tape comes in white, brown, and shades of green. It has a waxy feel, it stretches, and it's easy to tear by hand. As you wrap a stem wire with floral tape, the tape will stick to itself, giving the stem a smooth, lasting finish.

Wire

Suitable wire can be found wherever floral or craft supplies are sold. Wire is sold by the thickness, or "gauge" (the thinner the wire, the higher the gauge number).

Eighteen-gauge wire makes the perfect stem wire. Some craft supply companies manufacture an 18-gauge stem wire that is covered with paper. This type of wire is my favorite—it's great for making flower stems because the paper makes the wire thicker and more believable as a natural stem.

Twenty-two-gauge wire is perfect for the backs of petals and leaves. Look for white cotton–covered wire, which is easily colored to match the petal and leaf colors with markers.

Thirty-two-gauge cotton-covered wire usually comes in 10-yard (9.15 m) spools. You can find it in craft stores in green or white. This wire is helpful as a wrapping wire for making the flower centers and tying petals to the stem wire.

Tubing

When flower stems are visible in an arrangement (as with long-stemmed roses), it's a good idea to add girth to stems to make them seem more realistic. You can do this easily by slipping the stem wire into tubing and wrapping with floral tape. Your local pet shop with aquarium supplies will have a variety of silicone tubing. I find the 3/16"-diameter (0.5 cm) tubing is the best: it's the perfect size to create a realistic-looking stem, and it's soft, pliable, and very easy to use.

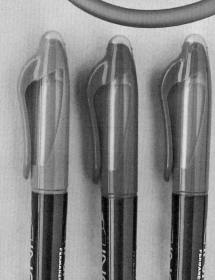

Paint and Markers

A few of the projects call for using paint to add details to the flowers. Any acrylic craft paint will work. Colored permanent markers are also an easy way to add details to your blooms or to color white wire to match the petals or leaves of your project.

Basic
Tools

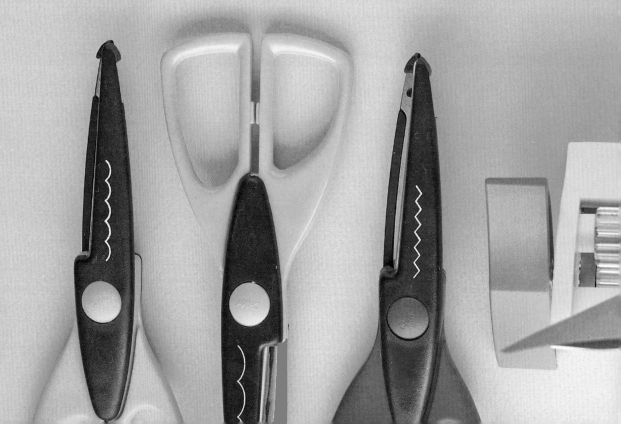

Scissors
Household scissors will be fine for the projects in this book. Smaller scissors can be useful for small cuts and details. Scrapbooking scissors made to create decorative edges (I especially like the scallop, pinking, and ripple ones), while not required for any of these projects, can be fun to experiment with to give your leaves and petals interesting edges.

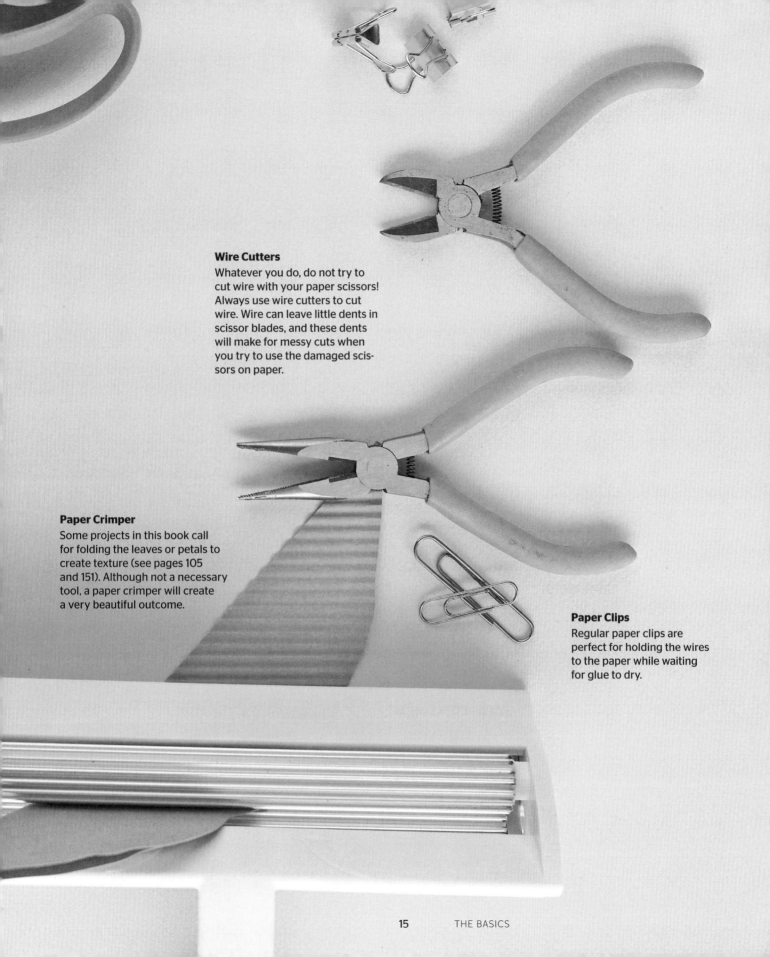

Wire Cutters

Whatever you do, do not try to cut wire with your paper scissors! Always use wire cutters to cut wire. Wire can leave little dents in scissor blades, and these dents will make for messy cuts when you try to use the damaged scissors on paper.

Paper Crimper

Some projects in this book call for folding the leaves or petals to create texture (see pages 105 and 151). Although not a necessary tool, a paper crimper will create a very beautiful outcome.

Paper Clips

Regular paper clips are perfect for holding the wires to the paper while waiting for glue to dry.

Common Techniques

Curling

Curling petals is easily achieved by folding the petal piece over a rigid cylinder-shaped tool, such as a pen, wooden skewer, or knitting needle. The smaller or tighter your desired curl, the thinner your tool should be.

Shaping Petals and Leaves

Some of the petals and leaves in this book require shaping to make the finished product look realistic. Most often these shaping techniques are simple—just folding or curling—however, some may be a little more involved. Here are some of the shaping techniques you will encounter.

Fan-Fold

This can also be called an accordion or zigzag fold. To make a fan-fold, start at one edge of the paper, fold the edge back, and crease. Turn the paper over, fold in the other direction, and crease. Continue turning the paper over, folding the edge back, and creasing to create a series of consecutive convex and concave folds. You can also use a paper crimper to create an interesting and tighter fan-fold look.

When working with leaf pieces, first fold the blade in half lengthwise. Beginning at the bottom of the leaf, fan-fold the entire piece on the diagonal. This will create a texture that resembles the veins in a leaf once the paper is unfolded.

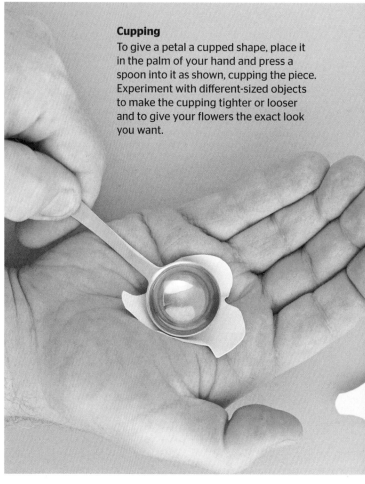

Cupping
To give a petal a cupped shape, place it in the palm of your hand and press a spoon into it as shown, cupping the piece. Experiment with different-sized objects to make the cupping tighter or looser and to give your flowers the exact look you want.

Crunching
Most often used for the carnation, this technique involves crunching the petal piece as if you were wadding a piece of trash, and then slowly opening the paper, leaving much of the creases intact.

Gluing

Here's the secret to gluing: don't overdo it! Just a small dab is all you need in most cases. If you've ever had those grooves or bumps show up on your craft projects, chances are you are using too much glue. Plus (an added bonus), the less glue you use, the faster the glue will dry. Using a brush is an easy way to keep from applying too much glue.

Wrapping with Floral Tape

To wrap a stem with floral tape, hold the end of a piece of tape against the end of the wire and twirl the stem, gently stretching the tape and overlapping as you work your way down the wire. Practice on a couple pieces of wire, and you will have the hang of it in no time.

Coloring Petals

You can create the marks or special coloring on flowers such as the dogwood, orchid, tiger lily, and pansy with markers or paint. It's best to do this before you shape or wire the petal.

Transferring Patterns

To keep the book intact, use tracing paper to trace the patterns and cut templates from card stock.

The patterns are all at their actual size, so there is no need to enlarge or reduce them. You can change the size of a pattern to make a larger or smaller flower by scanning the pattern into your computer and changing the scale in the print menu before printing it.

NOTE: If you alter a pattern piece, remember to change all the pattern pieces for the same flower by the same ratio.

Making Stamens

The center of almost every open flower requires a stamen and/or pistil of some type. you can make your own stamen by knotting one end of a 3" (7.6 cm) piece of heavily starched button thread and then dipping the knotted end of the thread in paint, creating a ball on the end when the paint dries. But that's a lot of work for something that can be found premade. I prefer to purchase artificial stamens and pistils: You can usually find them in the cake-decorating section of your neighborhood craft store or millinery-supply shop, or online. If necessary, it's easy to adapt the color of store-bought stamens with paint or markers.

For the flowers that require a special stamen not readily available at craft stores, instructions for the stamen will be included with the project instructions.

Use 32-gauge wire to tie the stamens together and create the center for the flowers.

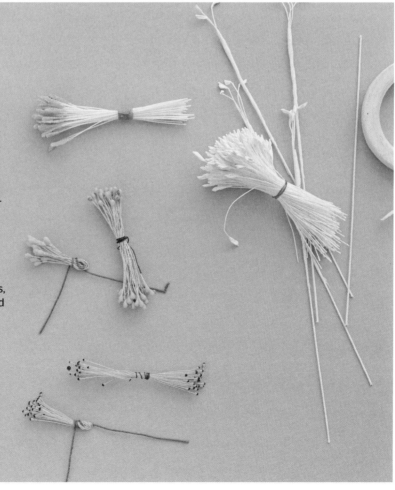

The Flowers

Now it's time to roll up your sleeves and get to work. Remember, it is only paper—don't be afraid to experiment. So many times people stifle their creativity by trying too hard.

Be free, have fun, and don't worry about making mistakes. Nothing in nature is perfect—in fact, it's the imperfections of nature that give it beauty.

MATERIALS

red paper

green paper

card stock

stem wire (18 gauge)

thin wire (22 gauge)

aquarium airline tubing

glue

floral tape

Trace the Red Rose patterns on page 162, and cut out the designated number of pieces for each pattern.

Red Rose

Since the rose is one of my favorite flowers, it's a perfect place to start.

I think Marie Osmond said it best when she lamented, "Paper roses, oh how real those roses seemed to be." Seriously though, if you are old enough to remember that song, don't start singing it now or you'll never get it out of your head . . . trust me.

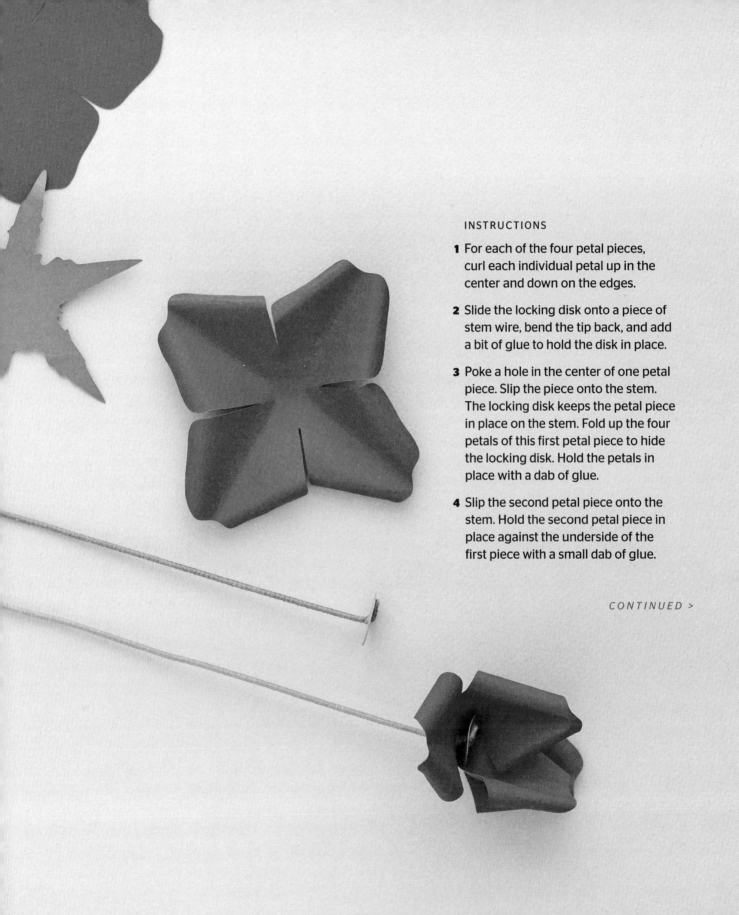

INSTRUCTIONS

1 For each of the four petal pieces, curl each individual petal up in the center and down on the edges.

2 Slide the locking disk onto a piece of stem wire, bend the tip back, and add a bit of glue to hold the disk in place.

3 Poke a hole in the center of one petal piece. Slip the piece onto the stem. The locking disk keeps the petal piece in place on the stem. Fold up the four petals of this first petal piece to hide the locking disk. Hold the petals in place with a dab of glue.

4 Slip the second petal piece onto the stem. Hold the second petal piece in place against the underside of the first piece with a small dab of glue.

CONTINUED >

5 Repeat step 4 for each of the remaining petal pieces.

6 Slip the second locking disk onto the stem, pushing it up to hold all petal pieces tightly together. Apply a dab of glue to keep it in place.

7 Slip the calyx onto the stem and slide it up to cover the locking disk, and glue it in place.

8 Slide the wire into a piece of aquarium airline tubing, and hold it in place with a dab of glue at the top under the calyx.

9 Wrap the tubing with floral tape, stretching and slightly overlapping the tape as you continue down the stem.

10 Fold each leaf in half and fan-fold it on the diagonal (see page 16). Glue a thin wire along the back spine of each leaf, leaving 3" (7.6 cm) of wire extending off the bottom for the petiole.

11 The leaf cluster closest to the flower consists of one large and two small leaves. Bundle the leaves and wrap the petioles together with floral tape to create this cluster.

12 Nip a small hole in the rose stem's tubing and slide the wire at the bottom of the leaf cluster inside the hole. Add a dab of glue to hold it in place.

Sweetheart Rosebud

In England, where the rose is the national flower, superstition has it that petals falling from a freshly cut rose portend bad luck.

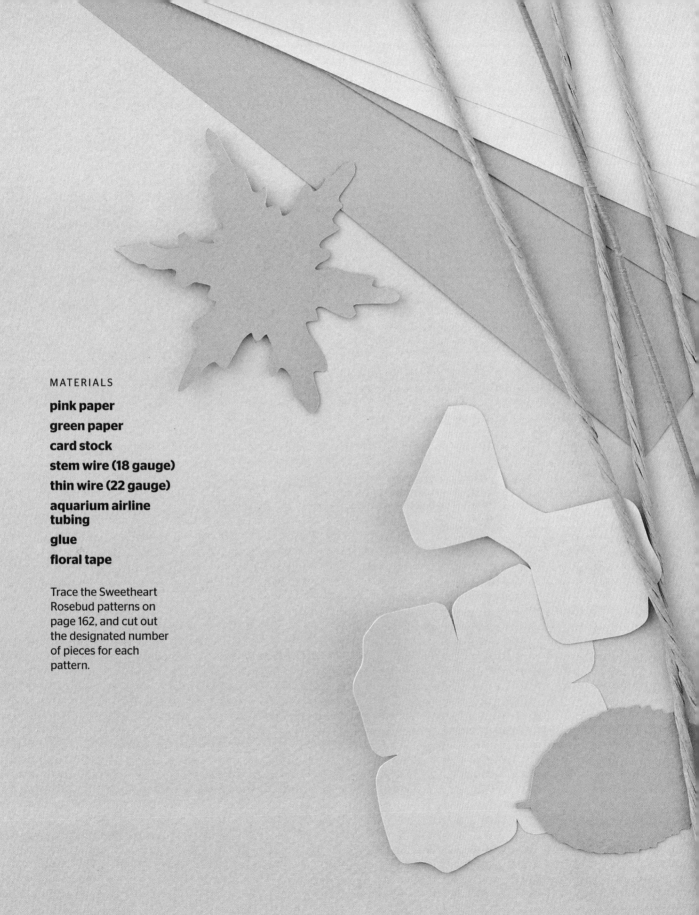

MATERIALS

pink paper

green paper

card stock

stem wire (18 gauge)

thin wire (22 gauge)

aquarium airline tubing

glue

floral tape

Trace the Sweetheart Rosebud patterns on page 162, and cut out the designated number of pieces for each pattern.

1 For each of the two petal pieces, curl each individual petal up in the center and down on the edges.

2 Fold the leaf in half and fan-fold it on the diagonal (see page 16). Open it and glue a thin wire along the back spine of the leaf, leaving 3" (7.6 cm) of wire extending off the bottom.

3 Slide the locking disk onto a piece of stem wire, bend the tip back, and add a bit of glue to hold the disk in place.

4 Poke a hole in the center of the #1 petal piece, and slip the piece onto the stem. The locking disk keeps the piece in place on the stem.

5 Roll up one petal of the #1 petal piece and hold it closed with a dab of glue.

6 Fold up the remaining #1 petals and hold them closed with a dab of glue.

7 Poke a hole in the center of the #2 petal piece, and slip the piece onto the stem.

8 Fold up the ends around the bud and glue them in place.

9 Slip the second locking disk onto the stem, pushing it up to hold all the pattern pieces tightly together, and apply a dab of glue to keep it in place.

10 Slip the calyx onto the stem and slide it up to cover the locking disk, and glue the edges up around the bud.

11 Slide the wire into a piece of aquarium airline tubing and hold it in place with a dab of glue at the top under the calyx.

12 Wrap the tubing with floral tape, stretching and slightly overlapping the tape as you continue down the stem.

13 Nip a small hole in the rose stem's tubing and slide the leaf into place. Add a dab of glue to hold the leaf in place.

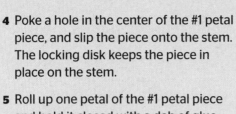

Carnation

Carnations date back to ancient Greece, where the botanist Theophrastus gave them their genus name Dianthus, meaning "the flower of God." They come in a variety of colors and can even be dyed.

Carnations are one of the most popular flowers in the world, mainly because they last a long time even after being cut. But they won't outlive these paper ones!

MATERIALS

pink paper

green paper

card stock

stem wire (18 gauge)

aquarium airline tubing

glue

floral tape

Trace the Carnation patterns on page 163, and cut out the designated number of pieces for each pattern. Tightly crunch (see page 17) the petal pieces, one at a time, and then gently reopen them.

INSTRUCTIONS

1 Fold one petal piece into quarters, and pinch the bottom to a point. Wrap the stem wire around the bottom of this, and add a dab of glue to hold it in place.

2 Punch a hole in the center of the second petal piece and slide it onto the stem. Add a dab of glue in the center to fix it to the previous petals.

3 Repeat step 2 for the remaining six petal pieces.

4 Slip the locking disk onto the stem, pushing it up to hold all petal pieces tightly together. Apply a dab of glue to keep it in place.

5 Slip the calyx onto the stem and slide it under the flower, and glue it in place.

6 Slide the stem wire into the aquarium airline tubing, and hold it in place with a dab of glue at the top under the calyx.

7 Wrap the tubing with floral tape, stretching and slightly overlapping the tape as you continue down the stem for approximately 3" (7.6 cm).

8 Place a leaf on either side of the stem, hold the leaves in place with floral tape, and continue to wrap the stem with the tape for another 3" (7.6 cm).

9 Repeat the leaf placement approximately every 3" (7.6 cm) down the stem.

10 Curl the leaves (see page 16).

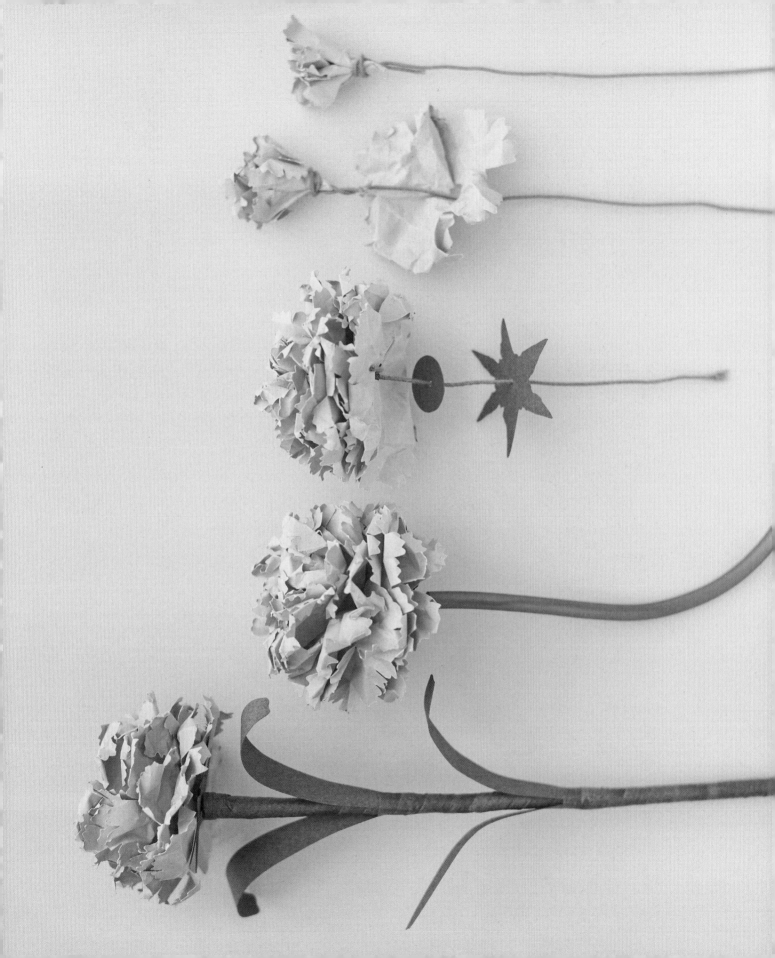

MATERIALS

white paper

green paper

thin wire (22 gauge)

stem wire (18 gauge)

green floral tape

stamens

glue

Trace the Easter Lily patterns on page 163, and cut out the designated number of pieces for each pattern.

Easter Lily

The Easter lily, as it's known in the United States, is native to the Ryukyu Islands in Japan. The Japanese imported the bulbs of *Lilium longiflorum* to the United States before the 1940s, but after the attack on Pearl Harbor, the supply was cut off and Easter lilies became so valuable they were called "white gold."

Easter lily bulbs need to be tricked, or "forced," into blooming for Easter by manipulating the temperature and light—but you can have these paper versions whenever you want them.

1 Glue a thin wire along the back of each petal piece, leaving 3" (7.6 cm) of wire extending off the bottom. Set aside for now.
NOTE: The lily leaves are not wired.

2 Bend the end of a thin wire into a loop, and cover it with floral tape. This will create the pistil. Attach it to the end of a stem wire with floral tape. Attach six stamens around the pistil, slightly lower than the pistil's tip. Hold them together by wrapping with floral tape.

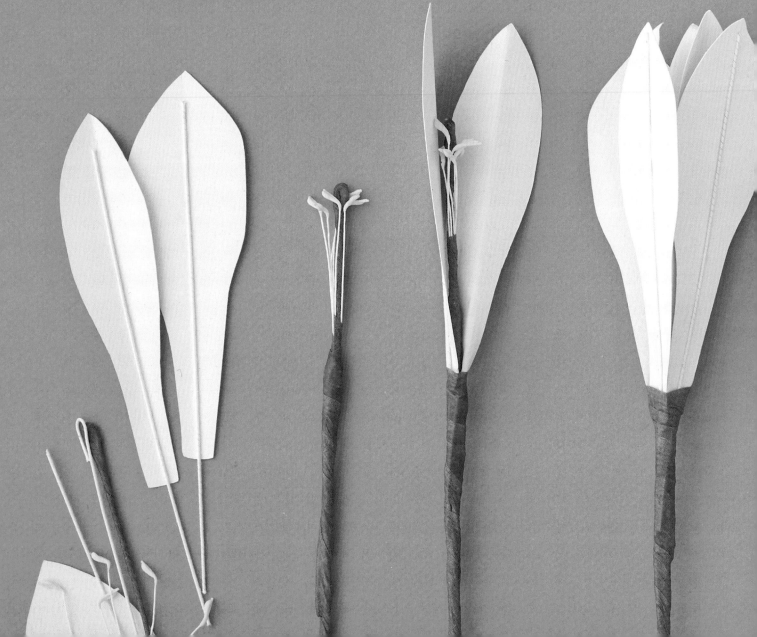

3 Place three #1 petals around the center stamens and pistil and hold them together by wrapping the wires with green floral tape.

4 Place three #2 petals between the #1 petals and hold them together by wrapping with green floral tape.

5 Curve the tips of the petals back to expose the center.

6 Wrap the stem wire with floral tape, stretching and slightly overlapping the tape as you continue down the stem for approximately 2" (5.1 cm).

7 Place a leaf on the stem, hold it in place with floral tape, and continue to wrap the stem with the tape for another 2" (5.1 cm).

8 Repeat the leaf placement approximately every 2" (5.1 cm) down the stem.

9 Curl back the leaves so they fall open in a natural-looking manner.

MATERIALS

purple paper

green paper

card stock

thin wire (32 gauge)

stamen

glue

floral tape

Trace the Violet patterns on page 163, and cut out the designated number of pieces for each pattern.

Violet

A very popular flower, perhaps because of its gentle size and appearance, the violet is the state flower for Illinois, Wisconsin, New Jersey, and Rhode Island. It is also the national flower of Greece.

Napoleon and Josephine Bonaparte were passionate fans of the violet. Josephine wore violets on her wedding day, and on each anniversary, Napoleon gave her a violet bouquet. During Napoleon's exile, the French Bonapartists chose the violet as their emblem and nicknamed Napoleon "Corporal Violet, the little flower that returns with the spring."

Violets, as their name suggests, come in various shades of purple, but it's not uncommon to find blue, yellow, white, and cream ones.

INSTRUCTIONS

1 Fan-fold the petal pieces and the leaf (see page 16). Keep the petals pieces folded for now.

2 Glue a thin wire along the back spine of the leaf, leaving 3" (7.6 cm) of wire extending off the bottom.

3 Fold a 10" (25.4 cm) piece of wire in half. At the fold, wrap the stamens.

4 Slide on the petal pieces as shown, turning as you go.

5 After all the petal pieces are in place, twist the bottoms of the wires together.

6 Open the petal pieces.

7 Slide the calyx onto the twisted wires, and push it up against the bottom of the petals, using a dab of glue in the center to hold it in place.

8 Wrap the wires with floral tape, stretching and slightly overlapping the tape as you continue down the stem.

9 Arrange overlapping leaves around the rim of a container. Arrange violets in clusters atop the leaves.

Dogwood

People often mistake the dogwood's four showy bracts for petals, but they are actually leaves. The flower is the tiny greenish-yellow part in the center.

Because the wood from dogwood trees is so hard, Native Americans used it to make arrows, and it has also been used to make numerous tools and even wedges to help split other woods. Christian legend has it that the cross on which Jesus was crucified was made from a dogwood tree. The flower's four leaves, arranged in the shape of a cross, each have a small indentation with a brown stain—which is supposed to represent a bloodstain made by a nail.

There is no better way to welcome spring than with a beautiful dogwood arrangement.

MATERIALS

white paper

green paper

thin wire (32 gauge)

stem wire (18 gauge)

stamen

**rust watercolor paint
or marker**

glue

green floral tape

brown floral tape

Trace the Dogwood
patterns on page 164,
and cut out the
designated number
of pieces for each
pattern.

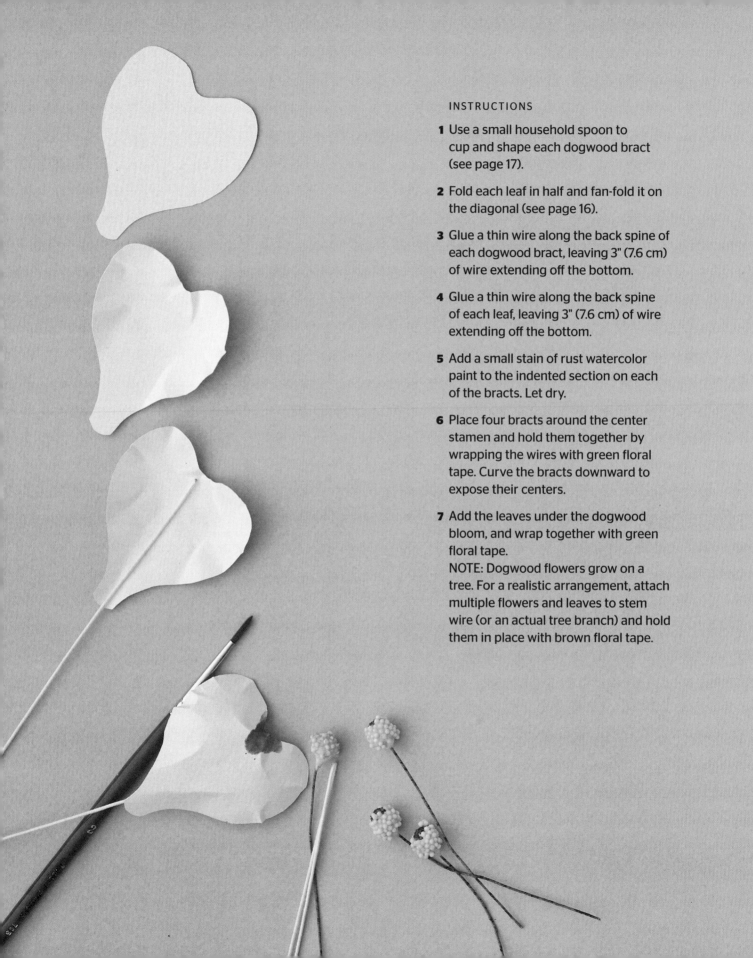

INSTRUCTIONS

1 Use a small household spoon to cup and shape each dogwood bract (see page 17).

2 Fold each leaf in half and fan-fold it on the diagonal (see page 16).

3 Glue a thin wire along the back spine of each dogwood bract, leaving 3" (7.6 cm) of wire extending off the bottom.

4 Glue a thin wire along the back spine of each leaf, leaving 3" (7.6 cm) of wire extending off the bottom.

5 Add a small stain of rust watercolor paint to the indented section on each of the bracts. Let dry.

6 Place four bracts around the center stamen and hold them together by wrapping the wires with green floral tape. Curve the bracts downward to expose their centers.

7 Add the leaves under the dogwood bloom, and wrap together with green floral tape.
NOTE: Dogwood flowers grow on a tree. For a realistic arrangement, attach multiple flowers and leaves to stem wire (or an actual tree branch) and hold them in place with brown floral tape.

MATERIALS

purple paper
green paper
card stock
stem wire (18 gauge)
thin wire (32 gauge)
glue
floral tape

Trace the Peony patterns on pages 164 to 168, and cut out the designated number of pieces for each pattern.

Peony

According to Greek mythology, the peony is named after Paeon, the physician to the gods. Peonies are large, beautiful flowers with many petals. It's said that mischievous nymphs hid within those petals on Mount Olympus.

Peony plants can live for hundreds of years, but they do not like to be disturbed. When a peony plant is moved or transplanted, it may not bloom again for several seasons. This version of the beautiful paper peony is not nearly as fussy.

INSTRUCTIONS

1 Glue a thin wire along the back spine of each leaf, leaving 3" (7.6 cm) of wire extending off the bottom.

CONTINUED >

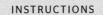

2 Loosely crunch the petal pieces, and then cup each petal (see page 17).

3 Slide the locking disk onto a piece of stem wire, bend the tip of the wire back, and add a bit of glue to hold the disk in place.

4 Slip the #1 petal onto the stem by poking a hole in the center of the piece. The locking disk keeps the pattern piece in place on the stem. Close up the petals to hide the locking disk and keep the pattern piece in place with a dab of glue.

5 Slip the #2 through #9 petal pieces on the same way, crinkling and cupping them to give then fullness. A dab of glue in the center of each petal piece near the stem will keep it in place.

6 Slip the second locking disk onto the stem, pushing it up to hold all the pattern pieces tightly together. Apply a dab of glue to keep it in place.

7 Slip the calyx onto the stem and slide it up to the bottom of the flower, and glue it in place.

8 Wrap the stem with floral tape, stretching and slightly overlapping the tape as you continue down the stem.

9 Insert the leaves 4" (10.2 cm) below the flower, and then continue with the floral tape down the remainder of the stem wire.

10 Create the peony bud by following the above instructions but omitting petal pieces #3, #4, #6, #8, and #9.

MATERIALS

white paper
green paper
stem wire (18 gauge)
glue
floral tape

Trace the Gardenia patterns on pages 168 and 169, and cut out the designated number of pieces for each pattern.

Gardenia

The gardenia represents grace and secret love. In the American South it is a symbol of hospitality. It's considered good luck to give a gardenia to a man, and in nineteenth-century England, men would wear gardenia blooms on the lapels of their formal wear.

Gardenias grow as shrubs or small trees and are indigenous to Australia, Asia, and Africa. They can be very finicky and will turn brown if handled too much . . . but not this paper version.

CONTINUED >

INSTRUCTIONS

1 Fold the #1 petal piece into quarters and roll it into a tight tube.

2 Curl the edges of the #2, #3, and #4 petal pieces.

3 Fold each leaf in half and fan-fold it on the diagonal (see page 16).

4 Glue a thin wire along the back spine of each leaf, leaving 6" (15.2 cm) of wire extending off the bottom.

5 Insert a stem wire into the center of the rolled #1 petal piece, and add glue to hold it in place.

6 Poke a hole in the center of the #2 petal piece that's large enough to slip over the bottom of the rolled #1 petal piece. Use a couple of dabs of glue to hold the petal piece in place.

7 Repeat for the #3 and #4 petal pieces.

8 Slip the calyx onto the stem and slide it up to the bottom of the flower, and glue it in place.

9 Wrap the stem with floral tape, stretching and slightly overlapping the tape as you continue down the stem, occasionally slipping in a leaf.

MATERIALS

yellow paper

green paper

card stock

thin wire (32 gauge)

stem wire (18 gauge)

glue

floral tape

Trace the Chrysanthemum patterns on page 170, and cut out the designated number of pieces for each pattern.

Chrysanthemum

Chrysanthemums, also known as mums, grow in a wide variety of colors. The plant was named for the Greek words for "golden" and "flower."

Chrysanthemums were a favorite of China's noble class, and the poor were not permitted to grow them in their gardens. According to Feng Shui customs, the chrysanthemum is a symbol for an easy life and will bring happiness to your home. The Japanese believe a chrysanthemum petal in the bottom of a wine glass ensures a long and healthy life.

INSTRUCTIONS

1 Curl all petals upward.

2 Fold the leaf in half and fan-fold it on the diagonal (see page 16). Open it, and glue a thin wire to the back spine of the leaf, leaving 3" (7.6 cm) of wire extending off the bottom.

CONTINUED >

3 Slide one locking disk onto a piece of stem wire, bend the tip of the wire back, and add a bit of glue to hold the disk in place.

4 Slip one #1 petal piece onto the stem by poking a hole in the center of the pattern piece. The locking disk keeps the pattern piece in place on the stem.

5 Fold the petals upward to cover the locking disk and add a dab of glue where needed to keep in place.

6 Repeat with the second #1 petal piece.

7 Repeat with both #2 petal pieces, one at a time.

8 Repeat with both #3 petal pieces, one at a time.

9 Repeat with both #4 petals, one at a time.

10 Slip the second locking disk onto the stem, pushing it up to hold all the pattern pieces tightly together, and then apply a dab of glue to keep it in place.

11 Slip the calyx onto the stem and slide it up to cover the locking disk, and glue it in place.

12 Wrap the stem with floral tape, stretching and slightly overlapping the tape as you continue down the stem, adding in leaves as you wrap your way down the stem.

MATERIALS

yellow paper

green paper

thin wire (32 gauge)

stem wire (18 gauge)

stamens

floral tape

glue

Trace the Daffodil patterns on page 171, and cut out the designated number of pieces for each pattern.

Daffodil

Daffodils always bring a smile to my face as they make their appearance in early spring. Also known as the jonquil or narcissus, the daffodil is native to Mediterranean regions and Europe.

According to Greek mythology, Narcissus was a beautiful, proud young man who rejected anyone who loved him. After he spurned the nymph Echo and left her heartbroken, Nemesis, the goddess of revenge, cursed Narcissus so that he would fall in love with the first person he saw. Narcissus leaned over to drink from a pool of water, and fell so in love with his own reflection that he drowned. The narcissus flower grew at the edge of the water.

INSTRUCTIONS

1 Curl the top edges of the throat petal down as shown.

2 Glue a thin wire along the back spine of each of the six yellow daffodil petal pieces, leaving 3" (7.6 cm) of wire extending off the bottom of each.

CONTINUED >

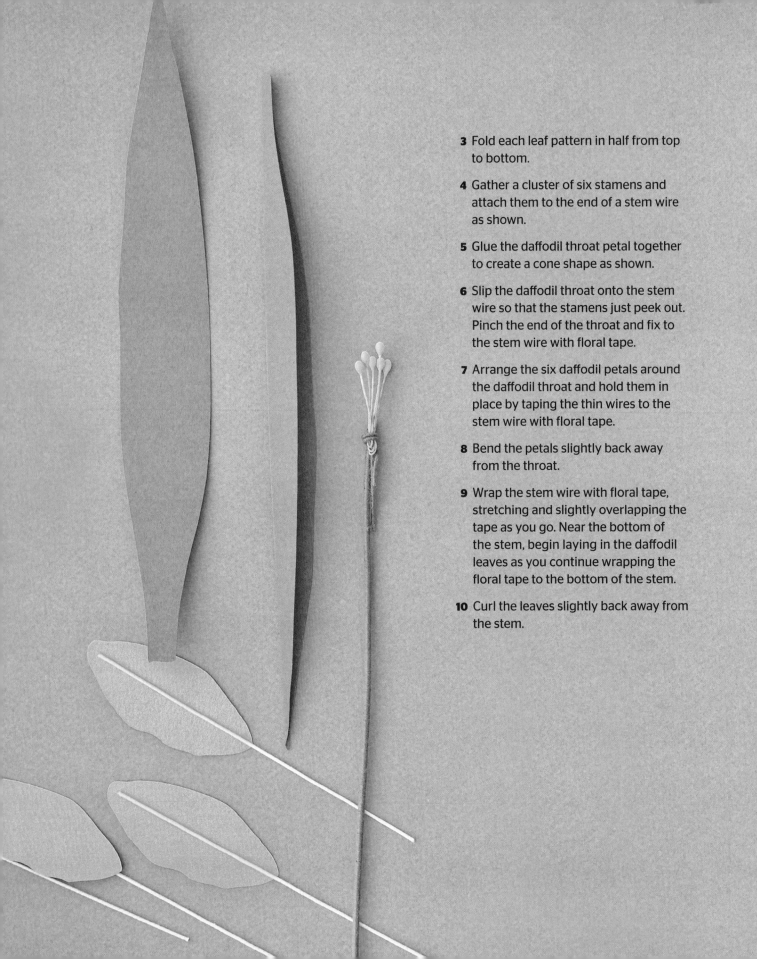

3 Fold each leaf pattern in half from top to bottom.

4 Gather a cluster of six stamens and attach them to the end of a stem wire as shown.

5 Glue the daffodil throat petal together to create a cone shape as shown.

6 Slip the daffodil throat onto the stem wire so that the stamens just peek out. Pinch the end of the throat and fix to the stem wire with floral tape.

7 Arrange the six daffodil petals around the daffodil throat and hold them in place by taping the thin wires to the stem wire with floral tape.

8 Bend the petals slightly back away from the throat.

9 Wrap the stem wire with floral tape, stretching and slightly overlapping the tape as you go. Near the bottom of the stem, begin laying in the daffodil leaves as you continue wrapping the floral tape to the bottom of the stem.

10 Curl the leaves slightly back away from the stem.

MATERIALS

yellow paper
green paper
light brown paper
card stock
stem wire (18 gauge)
thin wire (32 gauge)
brown felt
yellow craft sand
floral tape
glue

Trace the Sunflower patterns on pages 171 and 172, and cut out the designated number of pieces for each pattern.

Sunflower

Sunflowers are native to the Americas. One of the world's fastest growing plants, they can grow 10" to 12" (25.4 to 30.5 cm) in height in a single day.

The sunflower gets its botanical name Helianthus from the Greek words *helios*, meaning "sun" and *anthos*, meaning "flower." Sunflowers are so named because they turn their heads to follow the sun across the sky. These paper versions will need a little help with that.

INSTRUCTIONS

1 Crease the petals of the sunflower pieces and sunflower #1 calyx as shown.

2 Fold each leaf in half and fan-fold it on the diagonal (see page 16).

3 Glue the sunflower #2 calyx into a cup shape as shown.

4 Glue a thin wire along the back spine of each leaf, leaving 3" (7.6 cm) of wire extending off the bottom.

CONTINUED >

10 Slip the locking disk onto the stem, pushing it up to hold all the pattern pieces tightly together, then apply a dab of glue to keep it in place.

11 Slip the calyx cup onto the stem and slide it up to cover the locking disk, and glue it in place.

12 Wrap the stem with floral tape, stretching and slightly overlapping the tape as you go, and inserting leaves as you make your way down the stem.

5 Make a small loop in the stem wire, and glue it to the back of the card stock.

6 Glue the felt stamen to the front of the card stock, and fold back the edges to the back of the card stock, gluing them in place.

7 Mix glue into a tablespoon of yellow craft sand until it creates a thick paste. Stipple this mixture onto the brown felt. Let dry.

8 Slip one petal piece onto the stem and slide it up, pressing it against the back of the stamen. Use a dab of glue to hold it in place.

9 Repeat for the second and third petal pieces and then the light brown calyx piece.

MATERIALS

orange paper
green paper
card stock
stem wire (18 gauge)
thin wire (32 gauge)
floral tape
glue

Trace the Dahlia patterns on pages 173 to 175, and cut out the designated number of pieces for each pattern.

Dahlia

The dahlia is a native of Mexico, Central America, and Colombia. The Aztecs used to cultivate the dahlia for food and ceremonies. There are more than thirty species of dahlia, plus this one . . .

INSTRUCTIONS

1 Curl the petals of the #1 through #6 petal pieces.

2 Slide the locking disk onto a piece of stem wire, bend the tip of the wire back, and add a bit of glue to hold the disk in place.

3 Slip both #7 petal pieces onto the stem by poking a hole in the center of each piece. The locking disk keeps the petal pieces in place on the stem. Use a dab of glue to hold the top petal piece in place, and curl the petals of both pieces up to cover the locking disk.

CONTINUED >

4 Slip both #6 petal pieces onto the stem.

5 Repeat with both #5, #4, #3, #2, and #1 petal pieces. Slightly turn each piece so that the petals are not directly on top of each other.

6 Fold the leaf in half and fan-fold it on the diagonal (see page 16).

7 Glue a thin wire along the back spine of the leaf, leaving 3" (7.6 cm) of wire extending off the bottom.

8 Slip the second locking disk onto the stem, pushing it up to hold all the pattern pieces tightly together, and apply a dab of glue to keep it in place.

9 Slip the calyx onto the stem and slide it up to cover the locking disk, and glue it in place.

10 Wrap the stem with floral tape, stretching and slightly overlapping the tape as you continue down the stem.

11 Add the leaf approximately 4" (10.2 cm) below the flower and continue wrapping with floral tape to the bottom of the stem. NOTE: The Dahlia bud is created by omitting the #1 and #2 petals.

Trace the Lily of the Valley patterns on page 176, and cut out the designated number of pieces for each pattern.

MATERIALS

white paper
green paper
thin wire (32 gauge)
stem wire (18 gauge)
white floral tape
green floral tape
toothpick
cotton swabs
glue

Lily of the Valley

Even though the leaves and flowers are poisonous, the lily of the valley was at one time used for medicinal purposes. It was believed to restore speech and memory, and a sap made from crushing the plant was thought to promote common sense when spread on the forehead and the back of the neck.

According to a Christian legend, the lily of the valley has a very special meaning: the flower is said to have bloomed where the Virgin Mary's tears hit the ground at the crucifixion of Jesus.

Today the lily of the valley is thought to bring luck in love and, thus, is a very popular decoration at weddings.

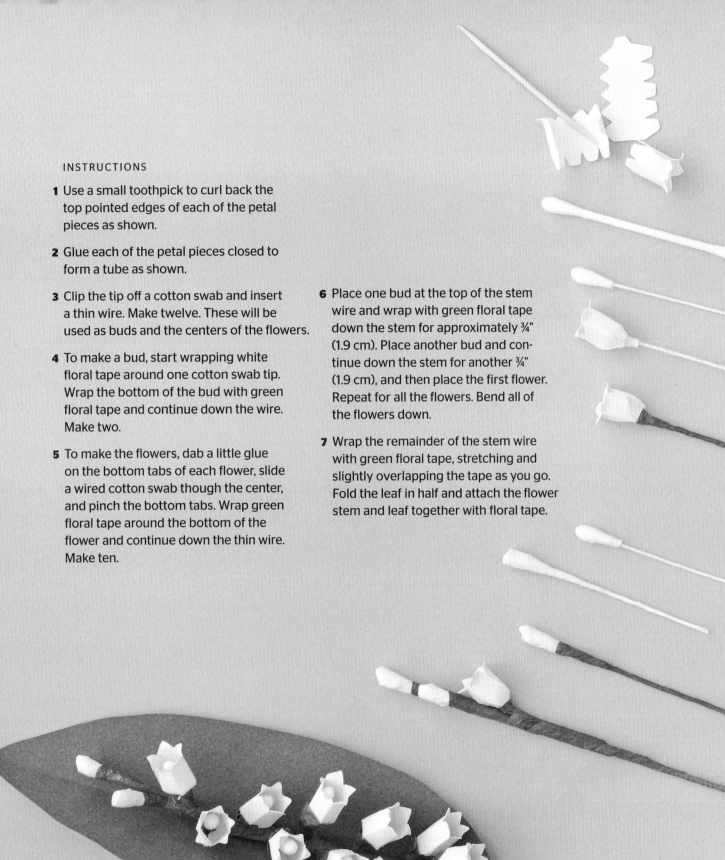

INSTRUCTIONS

1. Use a small toothpick to curl back the top pointed edges of each of the petal pieces as shown.

2. Glue each of the petal pieces closed to form a tube as shown.

3. Clip the tip off a cotton swab and insert a thin wire. Make twelve. These will be used as buds and the centers of the flowers.

4. To make a bud, start wrapping white floral tape around one cotton swab tip. Wrap the bottom of the bud with green floral tape and continue down the wire. Make two.

5. To make the flowers, dab a little glue on the bottom tabs of each flower, slide a wired cotton swab though the center, and pinch the bottom tabs. Wrap green floral tape around the bottom of the flower and continue down the thin wire. Make ten.

6. Place one bud at the top of the stem wire and wrap with green floral tape down the stem for approximately ¾" (1.9 cm). Place another bud and continue down the stem for another ¾" (1.9 cm), and then place the first flower. Repeat for all the flowers. Bend all of the flowers down.

7. Wrap the remainder of the stem wire with green floral tape, stretching and slightly overlapping the tape as you go. Fold the leaf in half and attach the flower stem and leaf together with floral tape.

yellow or white paper

green paper

card stock

stem wire (18 gauge)

thin wire (32 gauge)

yellow pipe cleaner

floral tape

glue

Trace the Daisy patterns on page 176, and cut out the designated number of pieces for each pattern.

Daisy

Ancient Celtic legend has it that God sprinkled daisies, made from the spirits of children who died at birth, all over the earth to cheer up grieving parents. This is why the daisy often symbolizes innocence.

One old wives' tale says that children will stunt their growth if they eat the root of a daisy, but another says if you eat three daisies after a tooth is pulled, you'll never have another toothache. It's also believed that Henry VIII would eat bowlfuls of daisies to relieve pain from his ulcers.

The French game *effeuiller la marguerite* translates literally to "rip off the daisy's leaves." This game is better known to us as "he loves me, he loves me not."

INSTRUCTIONS

1 Curl the edges of the petal pieces.

2 Fold the leaf in half and fan-fold jt on the diagonal (see page 16).

3 Glue a thin wire along the back spine of the leaf, leaving 3" (7.6 cm) of wire extending off the bottom.

4 Make the stamen by curling a yellow pipe cleaner into a flat disk as shown.

CONTINUED >

5 Slide the locking disk onto a piece of stem wire, bend the tip of the wire back, and apply a dab of glue to hold the disk in place.

6 Slip the first set of petals onto the stem by poking a hole in the center of the petal piece. The locking disk keeps the petal piece in place on the stem.

7 Repeat for the second and third petal pieces.

8 Slip the second locking disk onto the stem, pushing it up to hold all the petal pieces tightly together, and then apply a dab of glue to keep it in place.

9 Slip the calyx onto the stem and slide it up to cover the locking disk, and glue it in place.

10 Glue the rolled pipe cleaner stamen over the front of the locking disk.

11 Wrap the stem with floral tape, stretching and slightly overlapping the tape as you go, inserting a leaf approximately 2" (5.1 cm) below the flower.

Hyacinth

purple paper

green paper

stem wire (18 gauge)

thin wire (32 gauge)

green floral tape

stamens

glue

Trace the Hyacinth patterns on page 177, and cut out the designated number of pieces for each pattern.

In Greek legend, Hyacinthus was a beautiful young man and the favorite companion of Apollo. Zephyr, the West Wind, was also attracted to Hyacinthus and was jealous of his attraction to Apollo. One day, Zephyr could not control his jealousy any longer: when Apollo threw a discus, Zephyr blew it back, striking Hyacinthus in the head. Apollo cradled Hyacinthus in his arms as he died and turned his drops of blood into hyacinth flowers.

1 Curl back the long edges of each of the petal pieces as shown.

2 Glue each of the petal pieces closed to form a tube as shown.

3 Wrap six stamens with a thin wire. Repeat with the remaining stamens to make forty bundles of six stamens each.

4 Slide one stamen bundle through a flower and pinch the tabs closed around the wire.

5 Wrap floral tape around the bottom of the flower and continue down the wire, stretching and slightly overlapping the tape as you go.

6 Repeat steps 4 and 5 with all of the flowers and stamens.

7 Create the center stalk with four stem wires held together with floral tape.

8 Beginning at the top of the stalk, attach one flower with floral tape, and then closely insert the remaining flowers as you work your way down the stalk with floral tape.

9 Bend the flowers down.

10 Fold the leaves in half and insert at the bottom of the stem. Wrap with floral tape.

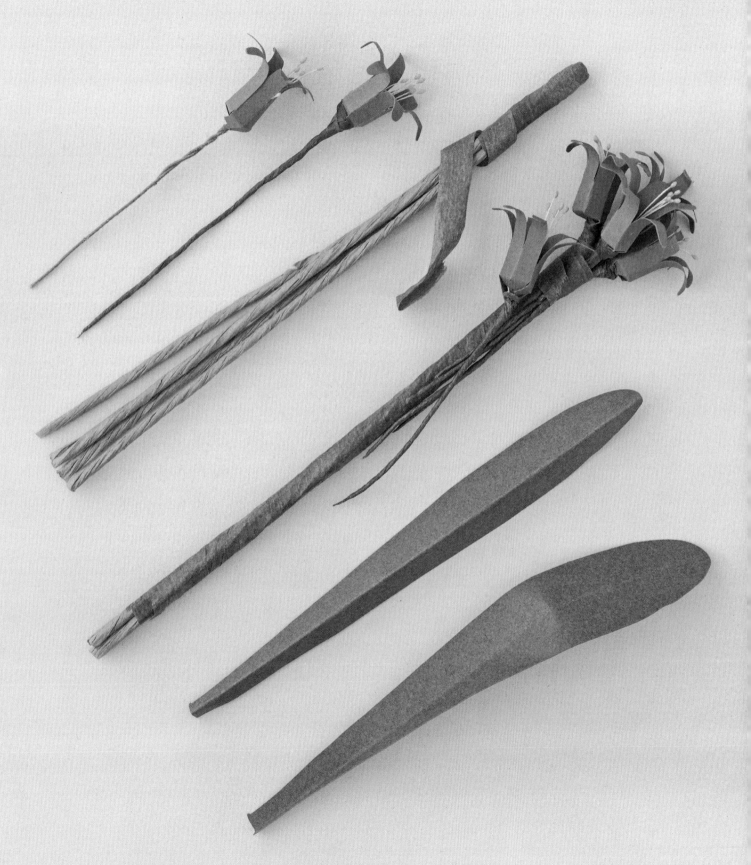

Lilac

According to Greek mythology, the beautiful nymph Syringa was running from Pan, the god of the forest, who was captivated by her beauty. Syringa was able to escape Pan's aggressive advances by turning herself into a lilac bush. Syringa is the lilac's botanical name.

The lilac is the state flower of New Hampshire and grows on a tree or shrub. The lilac tree is a symbol of new beginnings, and legend has it that the tree can protect your home from illness.

MATERIALS

purple paper

green paper

thin wire (32 gauge)

stem wire (18 gauge)

green floral tape

brown floral tape

stamens

glue

Trace the Lilac patterns
on page 177, and cut out
the designated number
of pieces for each pattern.

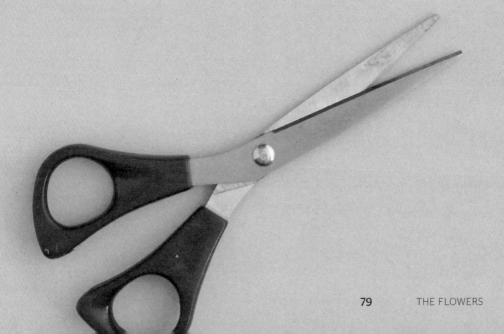

INSTRUCTIONS

1 Curl back the petal edges of each of the petal pieces as shown.

2 Glue each petal piece closed to form a tube as shown.

3 Fold three stamen pieces in half (creating six stamens) and wrap with a thin wire.

4 Slide the stamens though one flower, and pinch the tabs closed around the wire.

5 Wrap green floral tape around the bottom of the flower and continue down the wire, stretching and slightly overlapping the tape as you go.

6 Repeat steps 3 through 5 for all of the flowers.

7 Fold the leaf in half and fan-fold it on the diagonal (see page 16).

8 Glue a thin wire along the back spine of the leaf, leaving 3" (7.6 cm) of wire extending off the bottom.

9 Beginning at the top of the stem wire, attach one flower with brown floral tape, and insert the remaining flowers close together as you work your way down the stalk with floral tape.

10 After all the flowers are inserted and taped into place, insert the leaf, and continue with the brown floral tape to the bottom of the stem.

11 Bend the flowers down as shown.

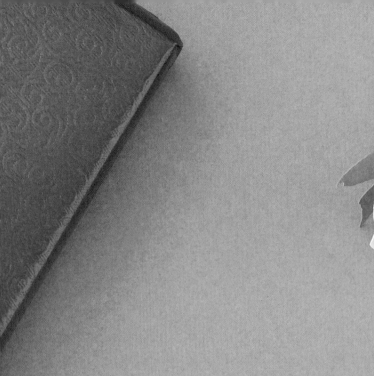

MATERIALS

pink paper

green paper

card stock

thin wire (32 gauge)

stamens

glue

green floral tape

brown floral tape

Trace the Apple Blossom patterns on page 177, and cut out the designated number of pieces for each pattern.

Apple Blossom

Apple blossoms symbolize good fortune and better things to come. They are the state flower for Michigan and Arkansas.

It is believed that the apple blossom has transformative qualities and can lift your spirits. The ancient Celts used apple blossoms as a symbol of fertility and decorated their bedchambers with the blooms.

INSTRUCTIONS

1 Fan-fold the petal pieces (see page 16).

2 Fold the leaf in half and fan-fold it on the diagonal.

3 Glue a thin wire along the back spine of the leaf, leaving 3" (7.6 cm) of wire extending off the bottom.

4 Fold a 10" (25.4 cm) piece of wire in half. At the fold, wrap the stamens.

5 Slide on the petal pieces as shown, turning as you go.

6 After all the petal pieces are in place, twist the bottoms of the wires together.

7 Open the petal pieces.

8 Slide the calyx onto the twisted wires, and push it up against the bottom of the petals, using a dab of glue in the center to hold it in place.

9 Wrap the wires with floral tape, stretching and slightly overlapping the tape as you continue down the stem.

10 To make a branch of apple blossoms, use stem wire (or even a small tree branch), and then affix multiple blossoms and leaves with brown floral tape.

MATERIALS

white paper
green paper
thin wire (32 gauge)
floral tape
stamens
glue

Trace the Water Lily
patterns on pages 177
and 178, and cut out the
designated number of
pieces for each pattern.

Water Lily

The water lily, an aquatic plant, can be pink, yellow, or
white. It has always served as an important symbol of
resurrection in Buddhist and Hindu religions, because
of the way many water lilies close their petals at night
and reopen them in the morning sun. Buddhists regard
the water lily as a symbol of enlightenment because the
beautiful flower emerges from mud.

INSTRUCTIONS

1 Glue a thin wire along the back spine of all the petal and calyx pieces, leaving 3" (7.6 cm) of wire extending off the bottom of each.

2 Gather thirty stamens and tightly wrap them together with wire.

3 Starting with the small petals, surround the stamen in a circular pattern, followed by the medium and then the large petals. Wrap with wire to hold everything together.

4 Wrap the bundle of wire with green floral tape.

5 Surround this bundle with the calyx pieces and hold them in place with another couple of layers of floral tape.

6 Starting on the outside, fold the calyx and petals down to expose the stamens.

7 Fold each leaf in half and fan-fold it on the diagonal (see page 16).

8 Glue a thin wire along the back spine of each of the leaves, leaving 3" (7.6 cm) of wire extending off the bottom of each.

9 To display your finished flower, wire the three leaves together and place the flower on top.

Purple Orchid

MATERIALS

purple paper
green paper
white acrylic paint
thin wire (32 gauge)
stem wire (18 gauge)
yellow pipe cleaner
glue
green floral tape
brown floral tape

Trace the Purple Orchid patterns on pages 178 and 179, and cut out the designated number of pieces for each pattern.

It is estimated that there are more than 25,000 different types of orchids existing in nature, and more being discovered each year. They are long lasting and elegant, and have historically symbolized wealth and beauty. To the ancient Greeks, the orchid was a symbol of virility; its Greek name *orchis* means "testicle."

INSTRUCTIONS

1 Using the photo for reference, paint the throat with the white acrylic paint. Let dry.

2 Curl the edges of the throat as shown.

3 Glue a thin wire along the back of the throat, starting 1" (2.5 cm) from the top and extending 3" (7.6 cm) off the bottom.

4 Glue the throat closed.

5 Glue a thin wire along the back spine of the #1 petal, the #2 petal, and the leaves, leaving 3" (7.6 cm) of wire extending off the bottom of each piece.

6 Fold a yellow pipe cleaner in half. Starting ½" (1.3 cm) from the fold, wrap the pipe cleaner (tightly) with brown floral tape, stretching and slightly overlapping the tape as you go. This will create a stamen for the orchid.

7 Slip the stamen into the orchid throat and hold it in place with green floral tape.

8 Surround the orchid throat with petals. Place one #1 petal at the opening of the throat and the remaining #1 petals behind the throat. The two #2 petals go to the left and right of the throat. Hold them in place with green floral tape.

9 Bend the petals open.

10 Orchids grow upside down (throat pointing down); use brown floral tape to affix the orchid to a stem wire in this position.

11 At the very bottom of the stem, slip in the orchid leaves and hold them in place with brown floral tape.

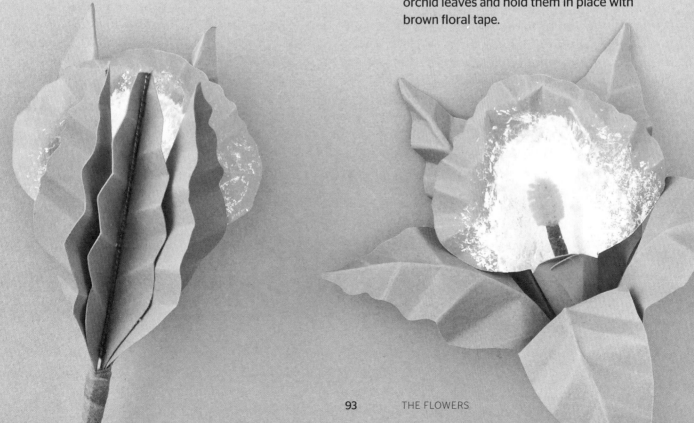

MATERIALS

yellow paper

green paper

white and purple acrylic paint

orange pipe cleaner

thin wire (32 gauge)

stem wire (18 gauge)

glue

green floral tape

brown floral tape

Trace the Yellow Orchid patterns on page 179, and cut out the designated number of pieces for each pattern.

Yellow Orchid

Many orchids have markings on the petals, some simple and some more elaborate, ranging from completely spotted to a glowing yellow in the center of the throat. If you wish, go ahead and have fun creating a newly discovered orchid by using acrylic paints to create your own pattern on the petals and throat.

INSTRUCTIONS

1 Using the photo for reference, paint the petals and the throat with the white and purple acrylic paint. Let dry.

CONTINUED >

2 Curl the edges of the orchid throat as shown.

3 Glue a thin wire along the back spine of petals #2 and #3 and the leaves, leaving 3" (7.6 cm) of wire extending off the bottom of each.

4 Glue a thin wire along the back spine of the orchid throat, starting 1" (2.5 cm) from the top and extending 3" (7.6 cm) off the bottom.

5 Fold an orange pipe cleaner in half. Starting ½" (1.3 cm) from the fold, wrap the pipe cleaner (tightly) with brown floral tape, stretching and slightly overlapping the tape as you go. This will create a stamen for the orchid.

6 Place the stamen in front of the orchid throat and hold it in place with green floral tape.

7 Surround the orchid throat with petals. Place one #1 petal at the opening of the throat and the remaining #1 petals behind the throat. The two #2 petals go to the left and right of the throat. Hold them in place with green floral tape.

8 Bend the petals open.

9 Orchids grow upside down (throat pointing down); fix the orchid to a stem wire with brown floral tape.

10 At the very bottom of the stem, slip in the orchid leaves and hold them in place with brown floral tape.

MATERIALS

purple paper

green paper

white and yellow acrylic paint

stem wire (18 gauge)

thin wire (32 gauge)

dark purple markers

yellow pipe cleaner

green floral tape

brown floral tape

glue

Trace the Phalaenopsis Orchid patterns on page 180, and cut out the designated number of pieces for each pattern.

Phalaenopsis (Moth) Orchid

The Phalaenopsis orchid is native to tropical Asia. It has clusters of various colored flowers and is one of the most popular orchids in the trade. Because of its shape, it is also known as the moth orchid. Easiest of all the orchids to grow, this orchid's blooms typically last from 80 to 120 days. Of course this paper version will last much longer.

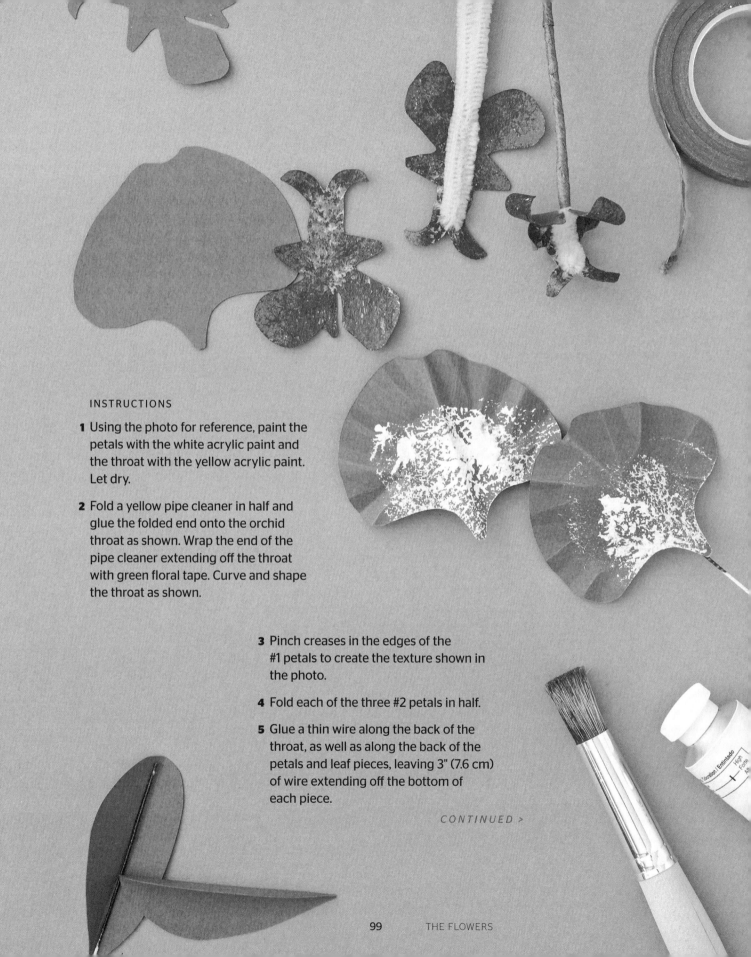

INSTRUCTIONS

1 Using the photo for reference, paint the petals with the white acrylic paint and the throat with the yellow acrylic paint. Let dry.

2 Fold a yellow pipe cleaner in half and glue the folded end onto the orchid throat as shown. Wrap the end of the pipe cleaner extending off the throat with green floral tape. Curve and shape the throat as shown.

3 Pinch creases in the edges of the #1 petals to create the texture shown in the photo.

4 Fold each of the three #2 petals in half.

5 Glue a thin wire along the back of the throat, as well as along the back of the petals and leaf pieces, leaving 3" (7.6 cm) of wire extending off the bottom of each piece.

CONTINUED >

6 Place the #1 petals on either side of the throat and hold them in place with green floral tape.

7 Place one #2 petal at the top of the flower and two #2 petals at the bottom as shown in the photos, and hold them in place with floral tape.

8 Orchids grow upside down (throat pointing down); fix the orchid to a stem wire with brown floral tape.

9 At the very bottom of the stem, add the orchid leaves and hold them in place with brown floral tape

Poinsettia

Poinsettias are native to Mexico. Legend has it that a poor Mexican girl on her way to church on Christmas Eve was crying because she had no gift to offer baby Jesus. An angel appeared to the girl and told her to gather weeds from the side of the road. By the time the girl arrived at the church, the weeds had turned to poinsettia flowers.

The red petals of the poinsettia are really bracts—the upper leaves of the plant. The actual poinsettia flower is the center green or yellow part. But to prevent confusion, we will refer to the red bracts as the petals and to the center part as the stamen.

MATERIALS

red paper
green paper
thin wire (32 gauge)
stem wire (18 gauge)
poinsettia stamen
green floral tape
glue
paper crimper

Trace the Poinsettia patterns on page 180, and cut out the designated number of pieces for each pattern.

INSTRUCTIONS

1 Fold all the petal and leaf pieces in half, and then crimp them on the diagonal.

2 Unfold all of the pieces, and glue a thin wire along the back spine of each, leaving 3" (7.6 cm) of wire extending off the bottom.

3 Create the center of the flower by tying a handful of yellow stamens to the stem wire.

4 Surround the center with petals in the following order:
#1, #2, #3, #1, #3, #2, #1, #2, #1, #3.
Place these side by side against the center, and hold them in place with a layer of floral tape.

5 Bend the petals open and shape them.

6 Wrap the stem wire with floral tape, stretching and slightly overlapping the tape as you continue down the stem.

7 Slip in the leaves approximately 3" (7.6 cm) below the flower and hold them in place with floral tape.

orange paper

green paper

thin wire (32 gauge)

stem wire (18 gauge)

pistil and stamens

aquarium airline tubing

orange marker (optional, see step 2)

green floral tape

glue

Trace the tulip patterns on page 181, and cut out the designated number of pieces for each pattern.

Tulip

While tulips are often associated with the Netherlands, they originally came from Turkey. There is a Turkish legend of a handsome prince named Farhad who was hopelessly in love with Shirin. Hearing that she had been killed and overcome with grief, he mounted his favorite horse and galloped off a cliff. According to the legend, a red tulip grew where each drop of his blood hit the ground, thus making this flower the symbol of perfect love.

INSTRUCTIONS

1 Shape the tulip petals by loosely curling them upward.

2 Glue a thin wire along the top (or inside) of each petal (as shown), leaving 3" (7.6 cm) of wire extending off the bottom. NOTE: White wire can be easily colored with a marker (orange in this example) to match the petals.

3 Bend the bottom of the petals as shown.

4 Fold each leaf in half from top to bottom, and glue a thin wire along the center, extending about 3" (7.6 cm) off the bottom.

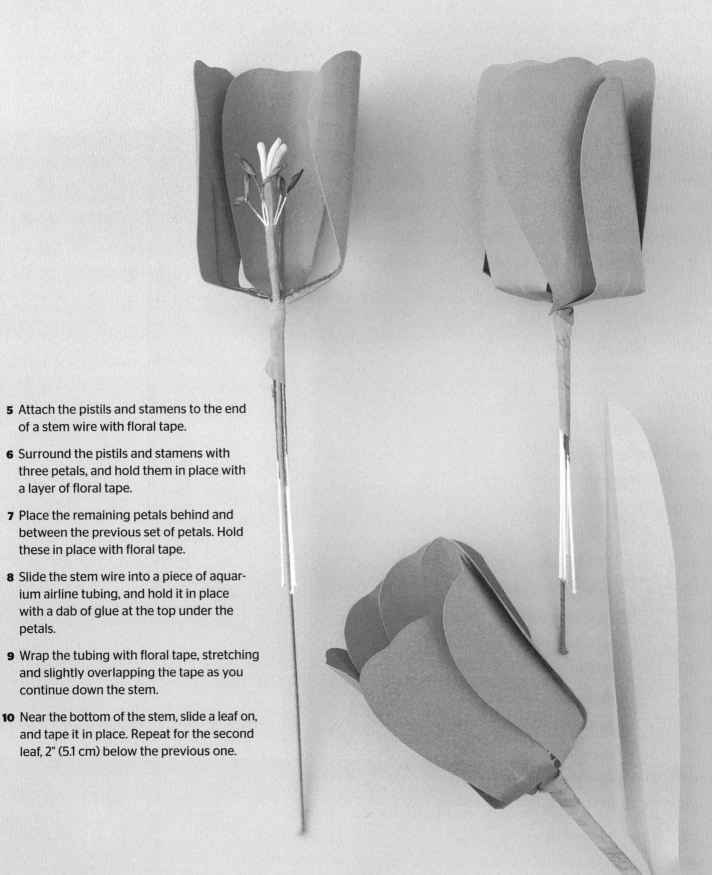

5 Attach the pistils and stamens to the end of a stem wire with floral tape.

6 Surround the pistils and stamens with three petals, and hold them in place with a layer of floral tape.

7 Place the remaining petals behind and between the previous set of petals. Hold these in place with floral tape.

8 Slide the stem wire into a piece of aquarium airline tubing, and hold it in place with a dab of glue at the top under the petals.

9 Wrap the tubing with floral tape, stretching and slightly overlapping the tape as you continue down the stem.

10 Near the bottom of the stem, slide a leaf on, and tape it in place. Repeat for the second leaf, 2" (5.1 cm) below the previous one.

Calla Lily

Calla lilies are native to South Africa, where they grow in abundance. The calla lily will bloom year-round as long as it has enough water, light, and nutrients. According to Greek mythology, calla lilies sprang up where the breast milk from the goddess Hera spilled on the earth.

A Georgia O'Keeffe painting of a calla lily sold at an auction in New York City for over six million dollars . . . just sayin'.

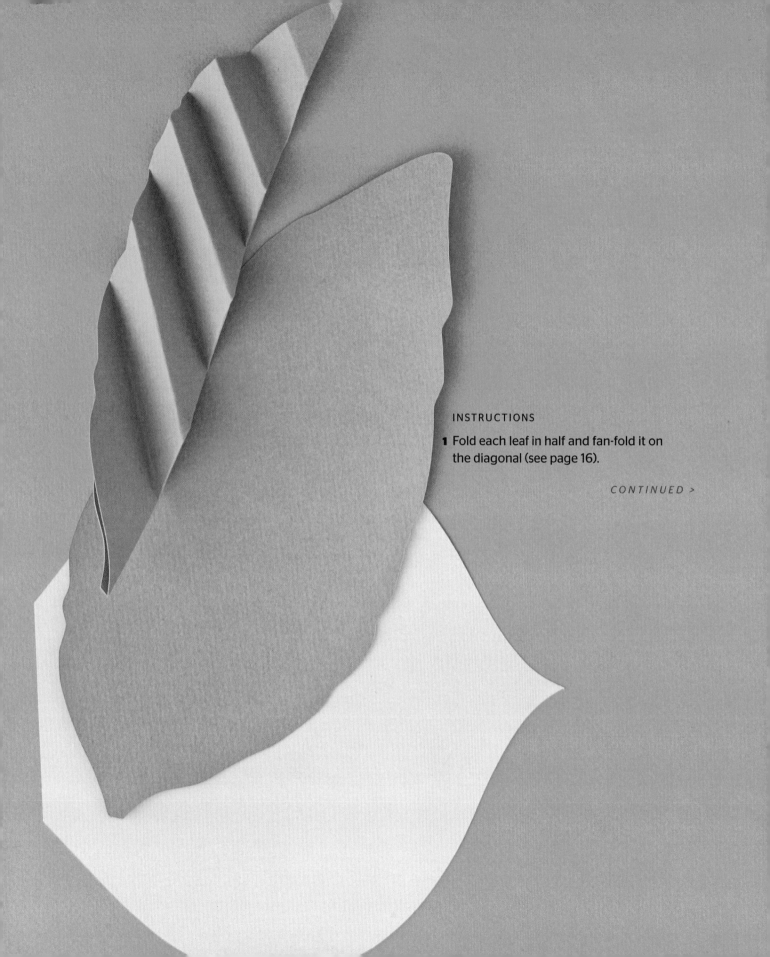

INSTRUCTIONS

1 Fold each leaf in half and fan-fold it on the diagonal (see page 16).

CONTINUED >

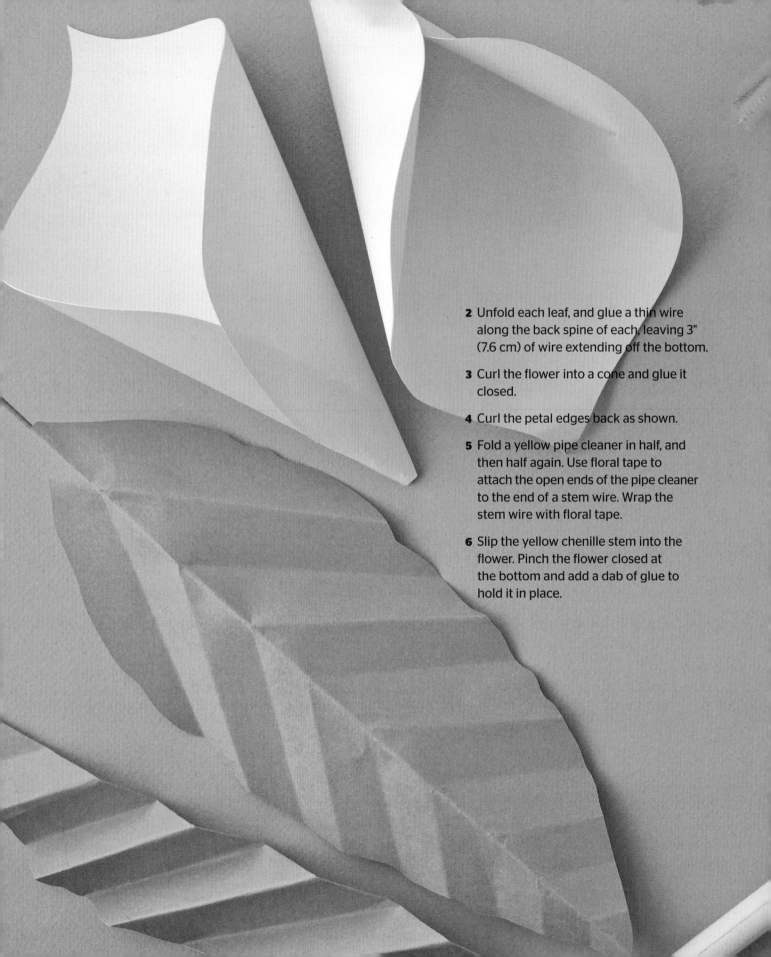

2 Unfold each leaf, and glue a thin wire along the back spine of each, leaving 3" (7.6 cm) of wire extending off the bottom.

3 Curl the flower into a cone and glue it closed.

4 Curl the petal edges back as shown.

5 Fold a yellow pipe cleaner in half, and then half again. Use floral tape to attach the open ends of the pipe cleaner to the end of a stem wire. Wrap the stem wire with floral tape.

6 Slip the yellow chenille stem into the flower. Pinch the flower closed at the bottom and add a dab of glue to hold it in place.

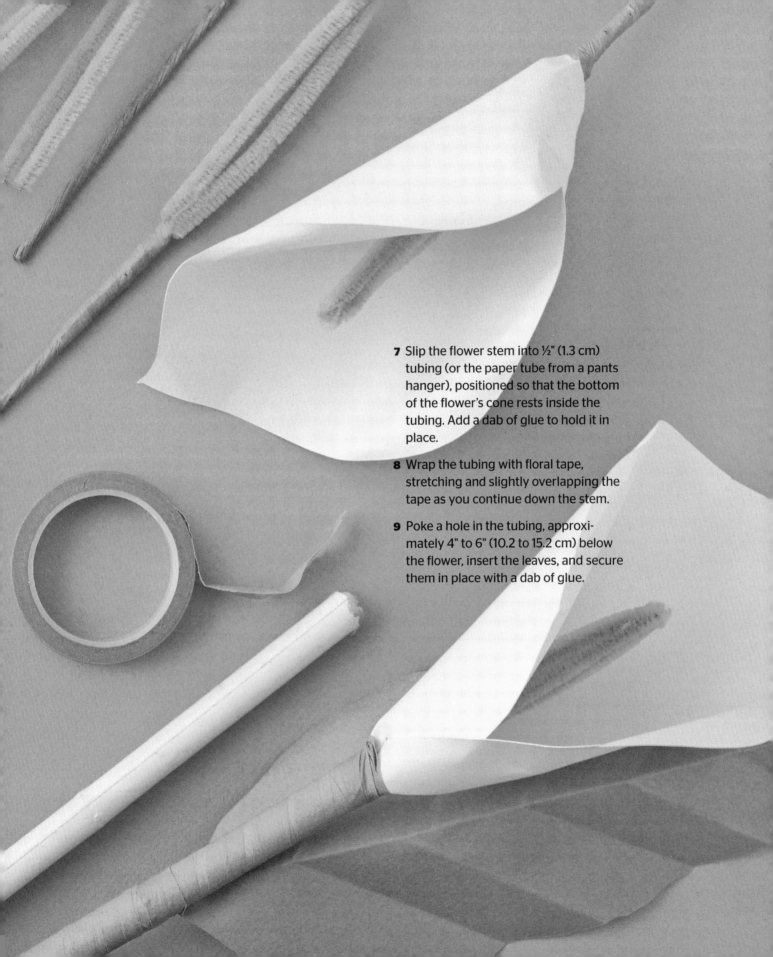

7 Slip the flower stem into ½" (1.3 cm) tubing (or the paper tube from a pants hanger), positioned so that the bottom of the flower's cone rests inside the tubing. Add a dab of glue to hold it in place.

8 Wrap the tubing with floral tape, stretching and slightly overlapping the tape as you continue down the stem.

9 Poke a hole in the tubing, approximately 4" to 6" (10.2 to 15.2 cm) below the flower, insert the leaves, and secure them in place with a dab of glue.

orange paper

green paper

thin wire (32 gauge)

stem wire (18 gauge)

stamens

aquarium airline tubing

brown and gray magic markers

green floral tape

glue

Trace the Tiger Lily patterns on page 183, and cut out the designated number of pieces for each pattern.

Tiger Lily

There is a myth that smelling a tiger lily will make you grow freckles—so watch out!

INSTRUCTIONS

1 Create the tiger lily freckles by randomly dabbing each petal front with a marker as shown.

2 Glue a thin wire along the back spine of each petal piece, leaving 3" (7.6 cm) of wire extending off the bottom. NOTE: The leaves are not wired.

3 Using the photo for reference, wire one large stamen to the end of a piece of thin wire to create the flower's pistil. Wire six small stamens about 2" (5.1 cm) below that, and hold them all together by wrapping with green floral tape.

CONTINUED >

4 Place three #2 petals around the pistil and stamens and hold them together by wrapping the wires with green floral tape.

5 Place three #1 petals between the #2 petals, and hold them together by wrapping with green floral tape.

6 Bend the petals open to expose the pistil and stamens.

7 Attach the tiger lily to the stem wire with floral tape.

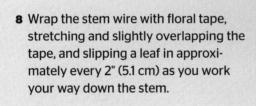

8 Wrap the stem wire with floral tape, stretching and slightly overlapping the tape, and slipping a leaf in approximately every 2" (5.1 cm) as you work your way down the stem.

9 Curl the leaves back so they fall open in a natural-looking manner.

purple paper

green paper

white acrylic paint

yellow pipe cleaner

thin wire (32 gauge)

stem wire (18 gauge)

stamens

aquarium airline tubing

floral tape

glue

Trace the Purple Iris patterns on page 183, and cut out the designated number of pieces for each pattern.

Purple Iris

The iris has a long history. In ancient Greece, purple irises were planted over the graves of women by grieving husbands. Drawings of irises can be found in Egyptian palaces, and during the Middle Ages, the iris represented the French monarchy. Eventually, the fleur-de-lis became the national symbol for France.

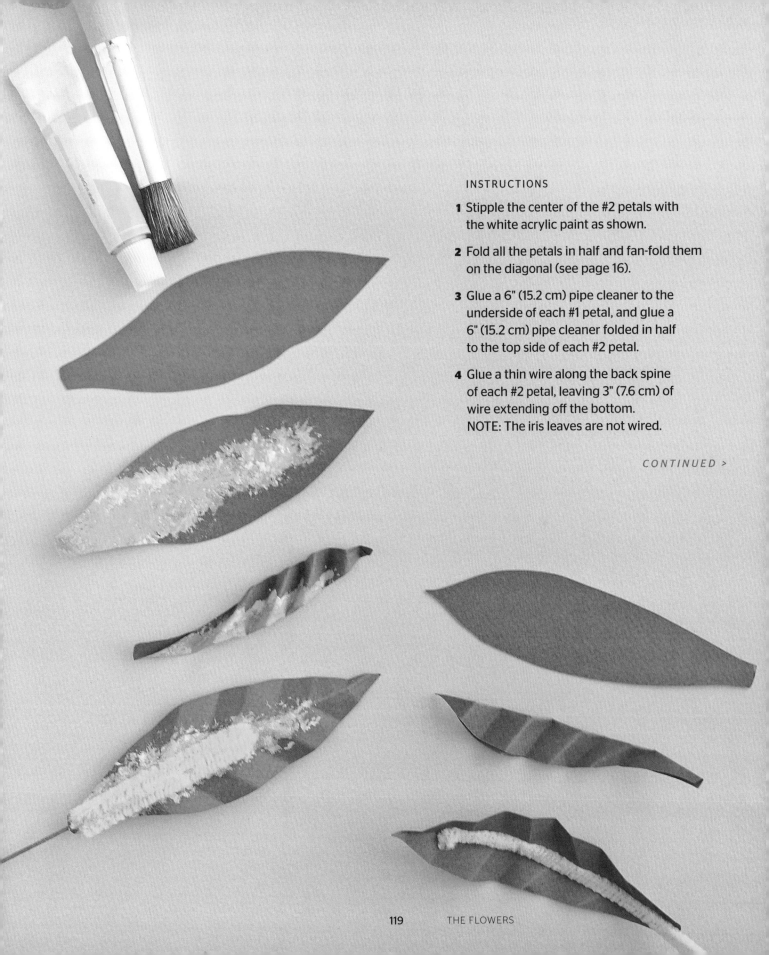

INSTRUCTIONS

1 Stipple the center of the #2 petals with the white acrylic paint as shown.

2 Fold all the petals in half and fan-fold them on the diagonal (see page 16).

3 Glue a 6" (15.2 cm) pipe cleaner to the underside of each #1 petal, and glue a 6" (15.2 cm) pipe cleaner folded in half to the top side of each #2 petal.

4 Glue a thin wire along the back spine of each #2 petal, leaving 3" (7.6 cm) of wire extending off the bottom.
NOTE: The iris leaves are not wired.

CONTINUED >

5 Wire three stamens together and secure them to the end of a stem wire with floral tape.

6 Shape the three #1 petals around the stamens and hold them together by wrapping the wires with green floral tape.

7 Place the three #2 petals between the #1 petals and hold them together by wrapping with green floral tape.

8 Bend the petals downward.

9 Slide the stem wire into a piece of aquarium airline tubing, and hold it in place with a dab of glue at the top under the flower.

10 Wrap the tubing with floral tape, stretching and slightly overlapping the tape as you continue down the stem.

11 Near the bottom of the stem, slide a leaf around the stem and tape it in place. Repeat for the second leaf, leaving 2" (5.1 cm) below the previous one.

12 Curl the leaves back so they fall open in a natural-looking manner.

White Iris

The iris represents faith, hope, and wisdom. There are more than 250 types of irises. The name comes from the Greek word for "rainbow," probably referring to the huge variety of colors the flower comes in.

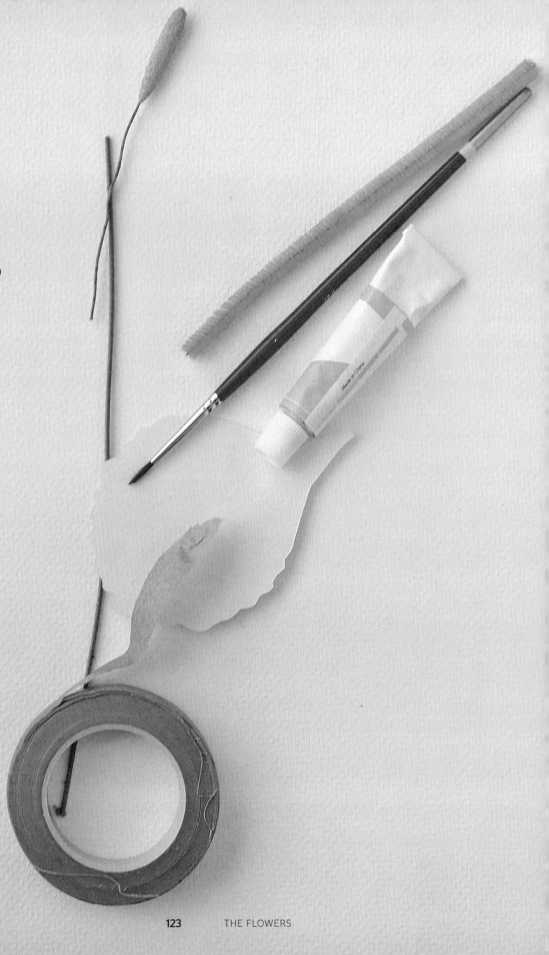

MATERIALS

white paper

green paper

yellow acrylic paint

orange or yellow pipe cleaner

thin wire (32 gauge)

stem wire (18 gauge)

yellow marker

aquarium airline tubing

large stamen

floral tape

glue

Trace the White Iris patterns on pages 183 and 184, and cut out the designated number of pieces for each pattern.

INSTRUCTIONS

1 Paint the center of each petal with watered-down yellow acrylic paint.

2 Fold a 6" (15.2 cm) pipe cleaner in half, and then glue it to one petal as shown. Repeat for the remaining petals. Wrap the part of the pipe cleaner that extends off the petal with floral tape.

3 Use a spoon to cup and shape each petal (see page 17). Curve each #1 petal up as shown so the pipe cleaner is inside the cupped petal. Curve the #2 petals down as shown so the pipe cleaner is exposed on the petal's surface.

4 Attach a large stamen to the end of a stem wire with floral tape.

5 Place three #1 petals around the center stamen and hold them together by wrapping the wires with green floral tape.

6 Place the three #2 petals between the #1 petals, and hold them together by wrapping with green floral tape.

7 Fold each leaf in half along its center.

8 Bend the #2 petals downward. Leave the #1 petals cupped around the center stamen.

9 Slide the wire into a piece of aquarium airline tubing, and hold it in place with a dab of glue at the top under the calyx.

10 Wrap the tubing with floral tape, stretching and slightly overlapping the tape as you continue down the stem.

11 Near the bottom of the stem, slide a leaf around the stem and tape it in place. Repeat for the second leaf, leaving 2" (5.1 cm) below the previous one.

12 Curl the leaves back to fall open in a natural-looking manner.

orange paper
green paper
thin wire (32 gauge)
stem wire (18 gauge)
center stamen
yellow stamen
glue
floral tape

Trace the California Poppy patterns on page 184, and cut out the designated number of pieces for each pattern.

California Poppy

The California poppy was declared the state flower of California in 1903. But it was the Spanish explorers who discovered and named the flower *cupa de ora*, or "cup of gold," many years before. California was known as the "Golden West" long before the gold rush because of these wildflowers.

INSTRUCTIONS

1 Use a spoon to cup and shape each petal (see page 17).

2 Glue a thin wire along the back spine of each petal and leaf, leaving 3" (7.6 cm) of wire extending off the bottom of each.

CONTINUED >

3 Wire twelve yellow stamens and a larger center stamen together and attach to a stem wire with floral tape.

4 Place the four petals around the stamens and hold them in place with floral tape.

5 Slip the calyx up the stem and under the petals, and glue it in place.

6 Wrap the stem wire with floral tape, stretching and slightly overlapping the tape and inserting the leaf as you work your way down the stem.

7 Bend the petals open.

MATERIALS

red paper
green paper
thin wire (32 gauge)
stem wire (18 gauge)
small black pom-pom
black stamens
glue
floral tape

Trace the Red Poppy patterns on page 184, and cut out the designated number of pieces for each pattern.

Red Poppy

Poppies, which can have four or six petals, have been known throughout history as a symbol for death and sleep: death because of the color and sleep because of the opium extract.

In Greek legend, Demeter, the goddess of corn, grain, and harvest, mourned because her daughter, Persephone, was abducted to the underworld; while Demeter mourned, famine covered the earth. Hypnos, the Greek god of sleep, made a drink from poppies for Demeter, and Hypno's drink induced sleep and healing so that while Demeter slept, the land would experience winter and when she awoke, spring.

Some farmers even today still plant poppies near their corn crop to ensure a good harvest.

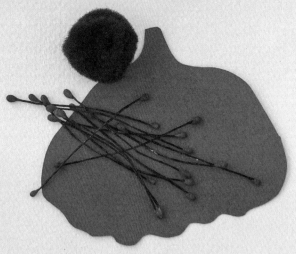

INSTRUCTIONS

1 Use a spoon to cup and shape each petal into a convex shape (see page 17).

2 Glue a thin wire along the back (concave) spine of each red petal and the back spine of each leaf, leaving 3" (7.6 cm) of wire extending off the bottom.

CONTINUED >

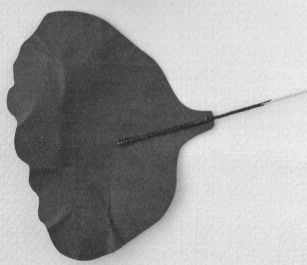

3 Bend a stem wire in half, trapping a black pom-pom in the crease. Twist the wire ends tightly, and wrap with floral tape. Wire a handful of stamens together with a thin wire and surround the pom-pom, holding it in place with green floral tape.

4 Surround the stamens with four petals and hold the petals in place with floral tape.

5 Bend each petal back gently.

6 Attach the flower to the stem wire and hold it in place with floral tape. Do the same with the leaves.

7 Wrap the stem with floral tape, stretching and slightly overlapping the tape as you continue down the stem.

MATERIALS

red paper

green paper

watercolor paint or markers

thin wire (32 gauge)

stem wire (18 gauge)

yellow stamens

yellow pipe cleaner

floral tape

glue

Trace the Hibiscus patterns on page 185, and cut out the designated number of pieces for each pattern.

Hibiscus

Traditionally, Hawaiian women would wear the hibiscus flower over their left ear (therefore, over their heart) to indicate that their heart was taken. A hibiscus bloom over the right ear meant the woman was available.

Hibiscus flowers come in various colors and color combinations. Often the petals have an ombre effect, going from dark in the center to lighter edges or vice versa. If you want a more colorful flower, feel free to experiment with paint or markers.

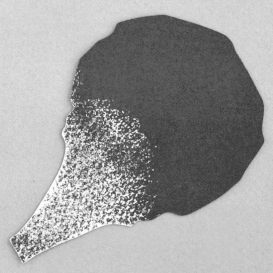

INSTRUCTIONS

1 Color the petals with paint or markers as desired. Follow the example here or experiment with your own design.

2 Use a spoon to cup and shape each petal into a convex shape (see page 17).

3 Glue a thin wire along the back (concave) spine of each petal and the back spine of the leaf, leaving 3" (7.6 cm) of wire extending off the bottom.

CONTINUED >

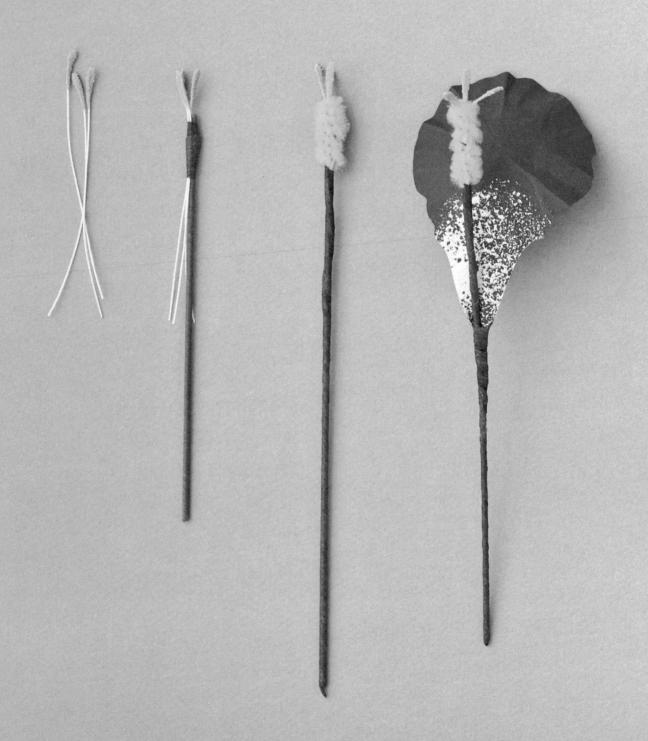

4 Attach three yellow stamens to the end of the stem wire with floral tape.

5 Cut a 3" (7.6 cm) piece of yellow pipe cleaner, and tightly wrap it around the wire, directly below the stamens as shown.

6 Attach the five petals 2½" (6.4 cm) below the chenille stamen, and hold them in place with floral tape.

7 Slip the calyx up the stem and under the petals, and glue it in place.

8 Wrap the stem wire with floral tape, stretching and slightly overlapping the tape as you go, and slipping leaves in as you work your way down the stem.

9 Bend the petals back gently to expose the stamens.

MATERIALS

purple paper

yellow paper

green paper

purple, red, and black markers or acrylic paint

thin wire (32 gauge)

stem wire (18 gauge)

yellow stamens

glue

floral tape

Trace the Pansy patterns on page 185, and cut out the designated number of pieces for each pattern.

Pansy

The pansy gets its name from the French word *pensée,* meaning "thought." It was believed to have magical powers, including curing a broken heart.

INSTRUCTIONS

1 Fold the leaf in half and fan-fold it on the diagonal (see page 16).

2 Shade the yellow petals using markers or acrylic paint. Let dry. Note that pansies come in many variations; feel free to experiment and develop your own.

3 Use a spoon to cup and shape each petal (see page 17).

4 Glue a thin wire along the back spine of each petal and leaf, leaving 3" (7.6 cm) of wire extending off the bottom.

CONTINUED >

5 Wire six stamens together and attach them to a stem wire with floral tape.

6 Place all three yellow petals around the center stamens and hold them together by wrapping the wires with green floral tape. NOTE: The #2 petal is the bottom of the flower.

7 Place both purple petals (slightly overlapping) behind the two yellow #1 petals, and hold all the petals together by wrapping with green floral tape.

8 Slip the calyx up the stem and under the petals, and glue it in place.

9 Wrap the stem wire with floral tape, stretching and slightly overlapping the tape as you go, and slipping leaves in as you work your way down the stem.

Sweet Pea

English gardeners call the sweet pea the "queen of annuals." It is a climbing plant native to the eastern Mediterranean. In 1699, a Sicilian monk named Franciscus Cupani sent sweet pea seed to England, where it was cultivated into the flower we have today.

MATERIALS

blue paper

green paper

stem wire (18 gauge)

thin wire (32 gauge)

floral tape

glue

Trace the Sweet Pea patterns on page 186, and cut out the designated number of pieces for each pattern.

INSTRUCTIONS

1 Use a spoon to cup and shape the #1 petal piece (see page 17) as shown.

2 Fold the #1 petal piece in half as shown, and glue a thin wire along the back spine, leaving 3" (7.6 cm) of wire extending off the bottom.

3 Curl the edges of the #2 petal as shown.

4 Glue a wire along the back spine of the #2 petal, leaving 3" (7.6 cm) of wire extending off the bottom.

CONTINUED >

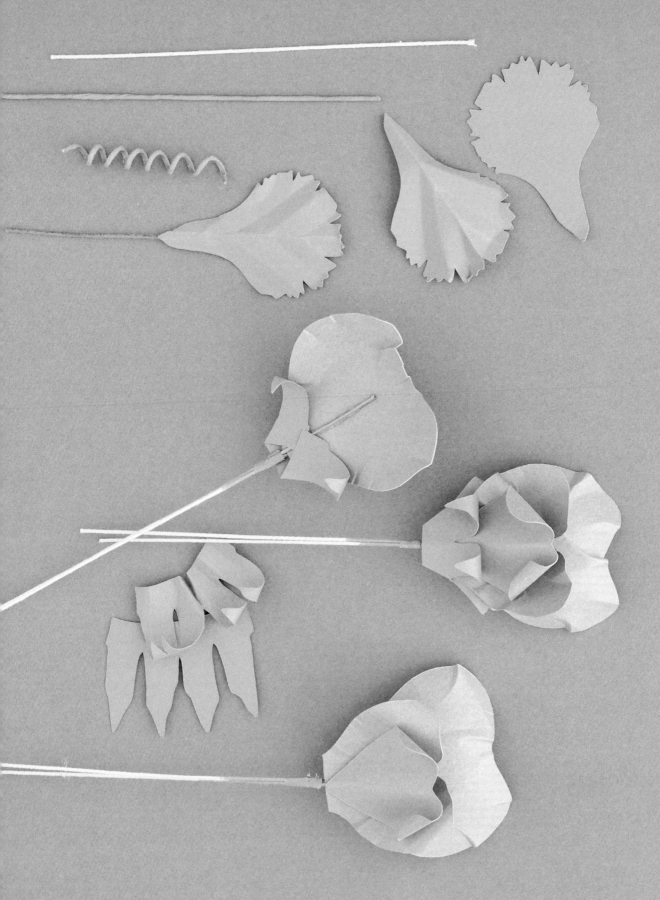

5 Place the #2 petal over the #1 petal and hold them together with a piece of floral tape.

6 Curl the tips of the calyx down, and then wrap the calyx around the flower, overlapping and gluing in the back as shown.

7 Fold the leaf in half and fan-fold it on the diagonal (see page 16).

8 Glue a thin wire along the back spine of the leaf.

9 Create the tendrils by covering a 6" (15.2 cm) length of thin wire with floral tape, and then wrapping the wire around a knitting needle or crochet hook.

10 Attach the flower, leaves, and tendrils onto a stem wire and wrap them with floral tape, stretching and slightly overlapping the tape as you continue down the stem.

MATERIALS

white paper

green paper

thin wire (32 gauge)

stem wire (18 gauge)

yellow pipe cleaners

glue

floral tape

Trace the Anthurium patterns on pages 186 and 187, and cut out the designated number of pieces for each pattern.

Anthurium

The anthurium is thought to protect against evil. It gets its name from the Greek for "tail flower." The heart-shaped flower is actually a spathe or leaf, while the spike, or "spadix," is where the tiny flowers grow. The anthurium's spathe can be yellow, white, pink, red, orange, or green. The flowers can grow as high as 20" (50.8 cm) and are popular for their long vase life of up to six weeks (but the paper version will last much longer).

1 Fold the petal in half and fan-fold it on the diagonal (see page 16).

CONTINUED >

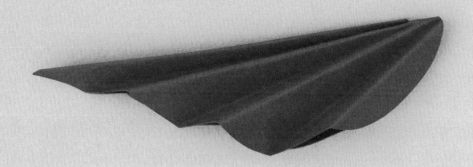

2 Fold the leaf in half and fan-fold it on the diagonal (see page 16).

3 Glue a thin wire along the back of the petal and the leaf, leaving 3" (7.6 cm) of wire extending off the bottom.

4 To make the stamen, first wrap a yellow chenille pipe cleaner around a stem wire as shown. When you get to the end of that pipe cleaner, wrap two pipe cleaners around the stem—this will make it look as if the stamen is getting thicker at one end.

5 Place the stamen up against petal stem, hold it in place with floral tape, and continue to wrap the remainder of the stem with floral tape, stretching and slightly overlapping the tape as you go.

6 Wire the leaf to a separate stem wire, hold it in place with floral tape, and continue to wrap the remainder of the stem, again stretching and slightly overlapping the tape as you go.

peach paper

green paper

thin wire (32 gauge)

stem wire (18 gauge)

yellow stamens

floral tape

glue

Trace the Gladiolus patterns on page 187 and cut out the designated number of pieces for each pattern.

Gladiolus

The gladiolus symbolizes remembrance, faithfulness, and honor. The flower gets its name from the Latin for "sword," because of the shape of its leaves. Gladioli represent strength—in ancient Rome, they were considered the flower of the gladiators.

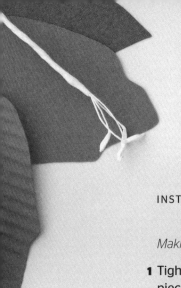

Bud #1

INSTRUCTIONS

Making the petal pieces and stamens

1 Tightly fan-fold or crimp all the petal pieces (see page 16).

2 Fold the leaf in half lengthwise.

3 Glue a thin wire along the back spine of each petal piece, leaving 3" (7.6 cm) of wire extending off the bottom.
NOTE: The gladiolus leaves and calyxes are not wired.

4 Wire three stamens together, and wrap them with floral tape. Repeat to make nine bundles of stamens in all.

Assembling the buds

BUD #1

5 Place three #1 petals around one stamen bundle, and hold them together by wrapping the wires with green floral tape.

6 Place three #2 petals between the #1 petals you assembled in step 5, and hold them together by wrapping them with green floral tape.

7 Place one #1 calyx and one #2 calyx on either side of the bud's base, and wrap them with floral tape. Curl each calyx down.

8 Bend the petals open fully to expose the stamens.

CONTINUED >

Bud #2

Bud #3

Bud #4

BUD #2

9 Repeat steps 5 though 7 to make a second bud, but this time bend the petals so the flower opens slightly less than bud #1.

BUD #3

10 Repeat steps 5 though 7 to make a third bud, but this time bend the petals so the flower opens slightly less than bud #2.

BUD #4

11 Place three #1 petals around one stamen bundle, and hold them together by wrapping the wires with green floral tape.

12 Place one #2 petal and two #1 petals between the #1 petals you assembled in step 11, and hold them together by wrapping them with green floral tape.

13 Place one #1 calyx and one #2 calyx on either side of the bud's base, and wrap them with floral tape. Curl the calyx down.

14 Bend the petals so the flower opens slightly less than bud #3.

CONTINUED >

Bud #5

15 Place five #1 petals around one stamen bundle, and hold them together by wrapping the wires with green floral tape.

16 Place one #1 calyx and one #2 calyx on either side of the bud's base, and wrap them with floral tape. Curl the calyx down.

17 Bend just the tips of the flower open.

BUD #6

18 Place two #1 petals around one stamen bundle, and hold them together by wrapping the wires with green floral tape.

19 Place one #1 calyx and one #2 calyx on either side of the bud's base, and wrap them with floral tape. Curl the calyx down.

20 Bend just the tips of the flower open.

BUD #7

21 Put two #1 petals around one stamen bundle, and wrap the wires with green floral tape.

22 Place one #1 calyx and one #2 calyx on either side of the bud's base, and wrap them with floral tape. Curl the calyx down slightly.

CONTINUED >

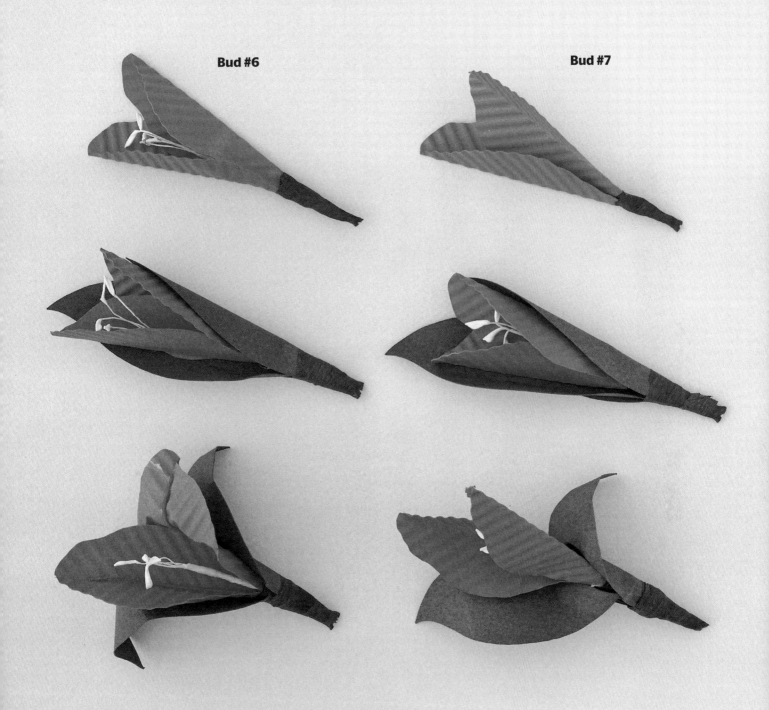

Bud #6

Bud #7

Bud #8

Bud #9

BUD #8

23 Roll one #1 petal around one stamen bundle, place one #1 calyx and one #2 calyx on either side, and then hold them together by wrapping them with green floral tape.

24 Bend the calyxes down slightly, but do not open the petal.

BUD #9

25 Roll one #1 petal around one stamen bundle, place one #1 calyx and one #2 calyx on either side, and then hold them together by wrapping them with green floral tape.
NOTE: Do not bend the calyxes or the petal open.

Assembling the gladiolus stalk

26 Beginning at the top right side of a stem wire, attach bud #9 with floral tape.

27 Below bud #9 and on the left side of the stem wire, attach bud #8 with floral tape.

28 Continue working your way down the stem, alternating the buds #7, #6, #5, #4, #3, #2, and #1.

29 Under bud #1, place two leaves on either side of the stem, and hold them in place with floral tape.

NOTE: Because this flower is a tall stalk, you may, at some point, need to work in another stem wire as you attach buds to add the length you need.

MATERIALS

red paper

orange paper

green paper

thin wire (32 gauge)

stem wire (18 gauge)

**½" (1.3 cm) tubing
(see Note)**

glue

floral tape

crimper

NOTE: Make the Bird of
Paradise stem with ½"
(1.3 cm) tubing or with
a paper tube off a pants
hanger from your local
dry cleaner.

Trace the Bird of Paradise
patterns on pages 188
and 189, and cut out the
designated number of
pieces for each pattern.

Bird of Paradise

The bird of paradise is also known as the crane flower
and is commonly viewed as a symbol of joy and freedom.
The flower originated in South Africa, where it grows wild.
It is thought to get its name from its shape, which resembles
the beak and head plumage of a bird.

INSTRUCTIONS

1 Fold all the petals in half lengthwise and crimp each one.

2 Glue a thin wire in the crease of each petal piece, leaving 3" (7.6 cm) of wire extending off the bottom.

3 Loosely roll the #1 leaf and the #2 leaf in half—do not make a hard crease.

CONTINUED >

4 Stack the petals together inside each other in the following order: #4, #2, #5, #1, #5, #5, #2, #4, #3, and #1. Tape the bottom wires together with floral tape.

5 Stick the above set of petals into the end of a piece of ½" (1.3 cm) tubing, and hold them in place with glue.

6 Attach base #1 and glue in place.

7 Attach base #2 and glue in place.

8 Wrap the stem with floral tape, stretching and slightly overlapping the tape as you go.

9 Fan the petals open.

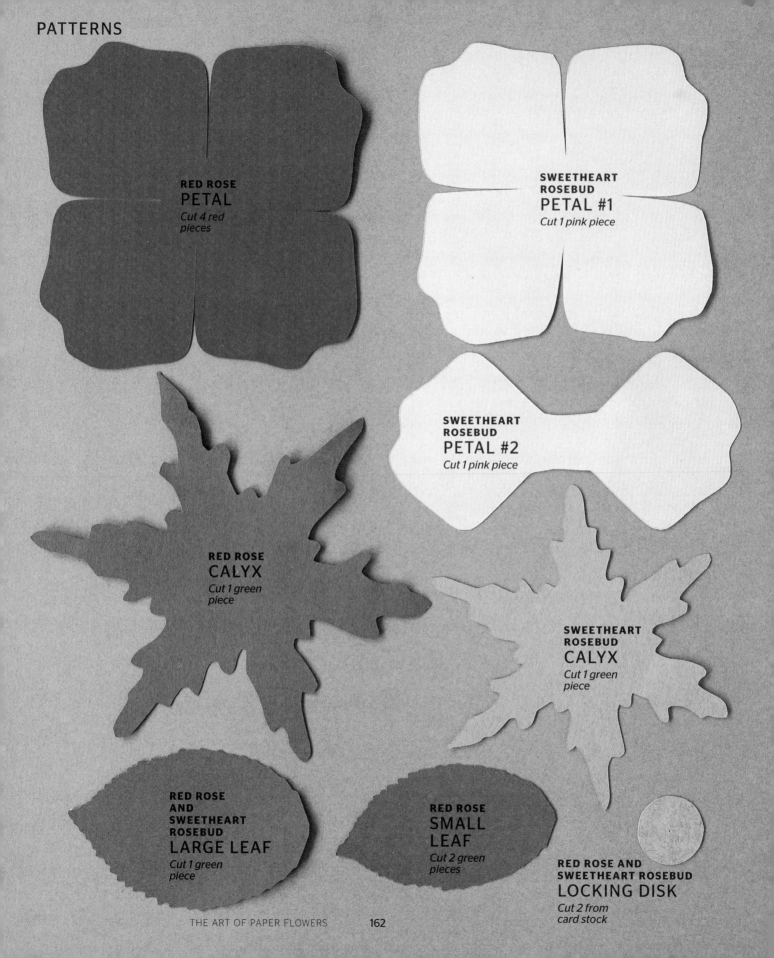

RED ROSE
PETAL
Cut 4 red pieces

SWEETHEART ROSEBUD
PETAL #1
Cut 1 pink piece

SWEETHEART ROSEBUD
PETAL #2
Cut 1 pink piece

RED ROSE
CALYX
Cut 1 green piece

SWEETHEART ROSEBUD
CALYX
Cut 1 green piece

RED ROSE AND SWEETHEART ROSEBUD
LARGE LEAF
Cut 1 green piece

RED ROSE
SMALL LEAF
Cut 2 green pieces

RED ROSE AND SWEETHEART ROSEBUD
LOCKING DISK
Cut 2 from card stock

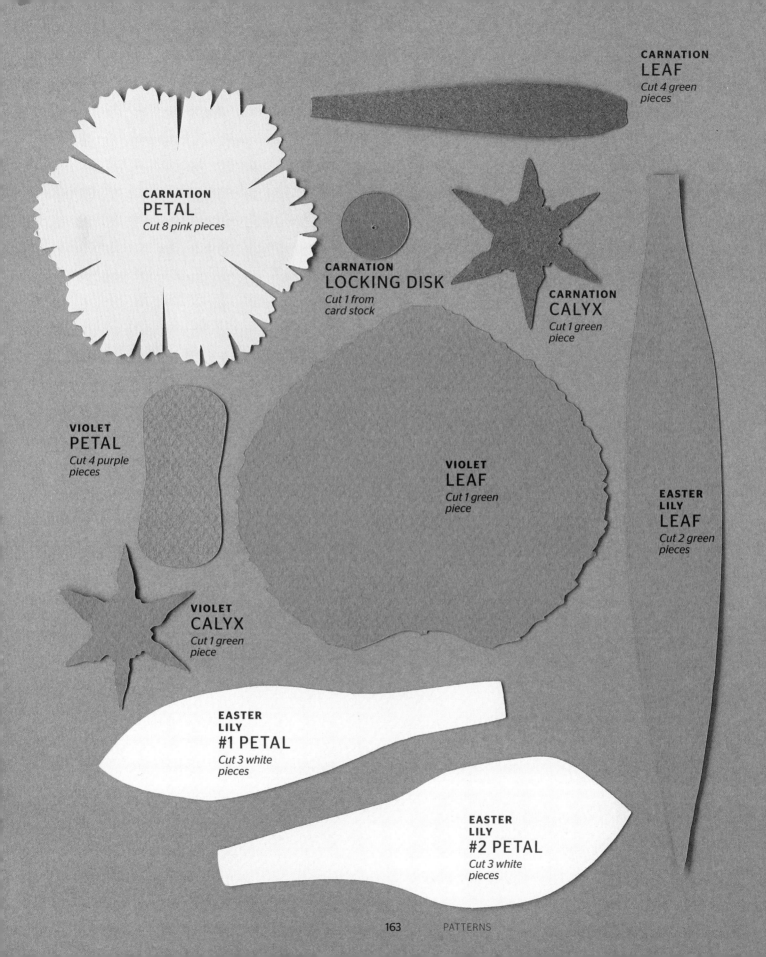

CARNATION
LEAF
Cut 4 green pieces

CARNATION
PETAL
Cut 8 pink pieces

CARNATION
LOCKING DISK
Cut 1 from card stock

CARNATION
CALYX
Cut 1 green piece

VIOLET
PETAL
Cut 4 purple pieces

VIOLET
LEAF
Cut 1 green piece

EASTER LILY
LEAF
Cut 2 green pieces

VIOLET
CALYX
Cut 1 green piece

EASTER LILY
#1 PETAL
Cut 3 white pieces

EASTER LILY
#2 PETAL
Cut 3 white pieces

DOGWOOD
LEAF

Cut 2 green pieces

PEONY
LOCKING
DISK

Cut 2 from card stock

PEONY
#3 PETAL

Cut 1 purple piece

PEONY
#2 PETAL

Cut 1 purple piece

PEONY
#1 PETAL

Cut 1 purple piece

DOGWOOD
PETAL

Cut 4 white pieces

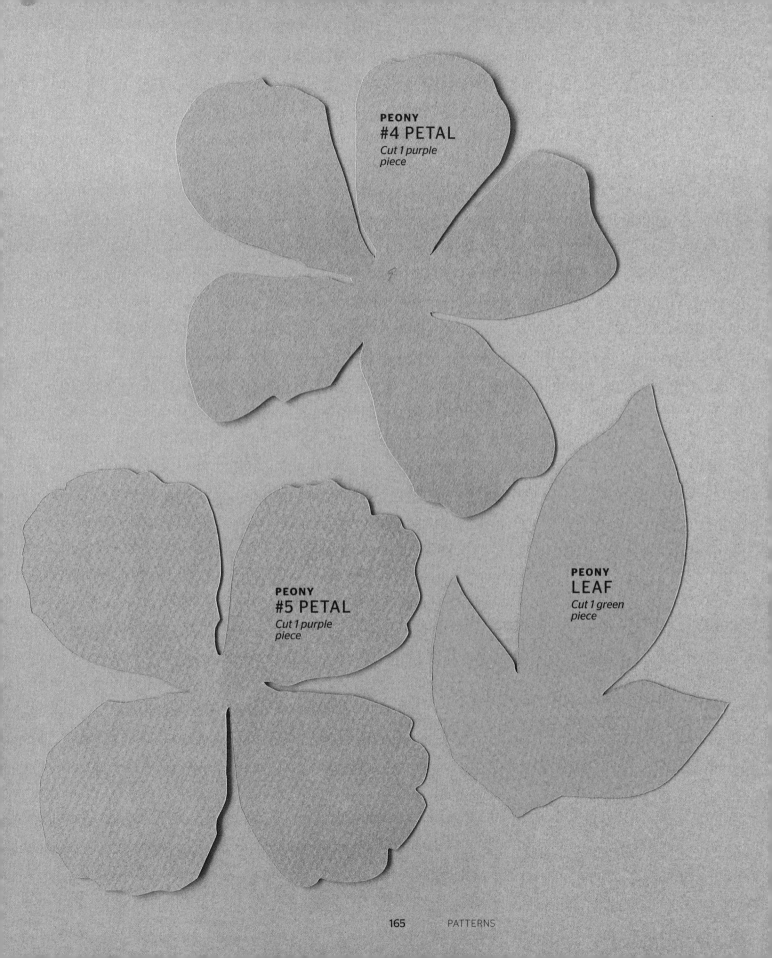

PEONY
#4 PETAL
Cut 1 purple piece

PEONY
#5 PETAL
Cut 1 purple piece

PEONY
LEAF
Cut 1 green piece

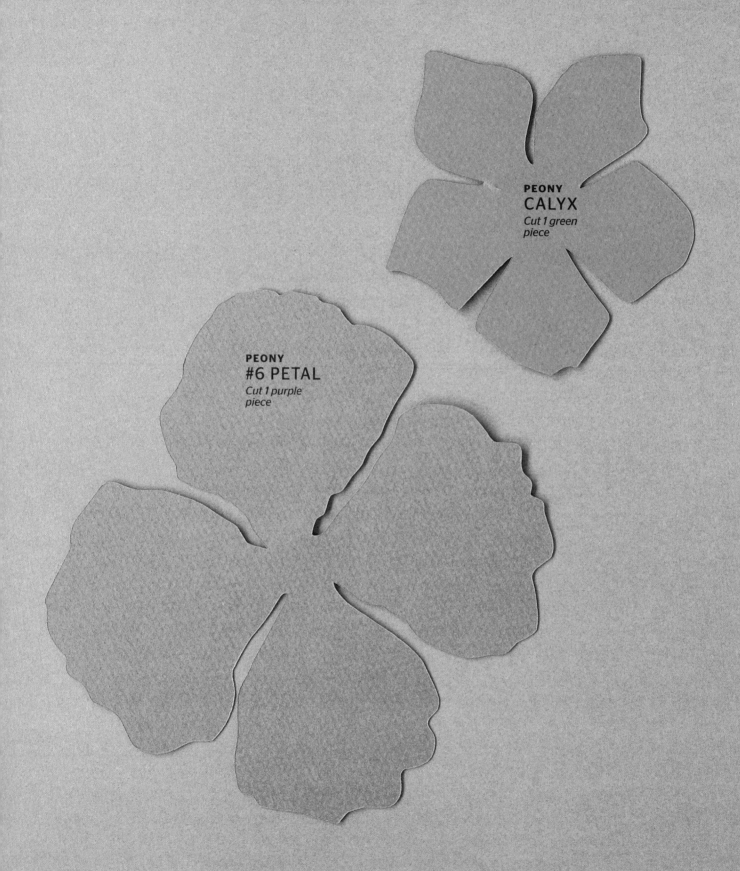

PEONY
CALYX
Cut 1 green piece

PEONY
#6 PETAL
Cut 1 purple piece

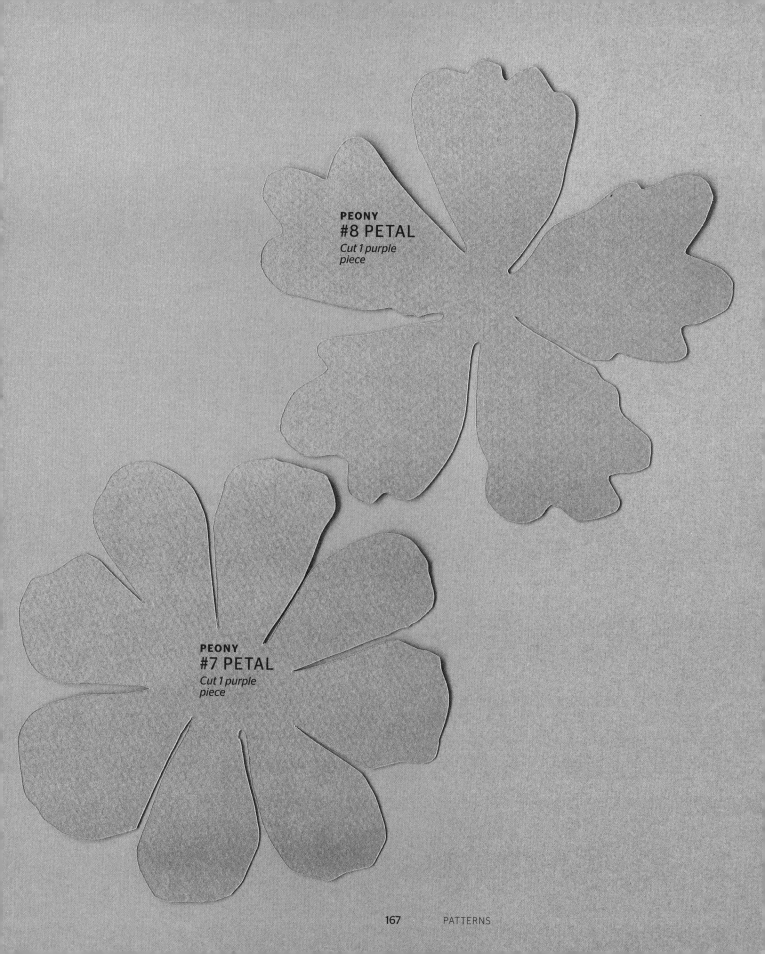

PEONY
#8 PETAL
Cut 1 purple piece

PEONY
#7 PETAL
Cut 1 purple piece

PEONY
#9 PETAL
Cut 1 purple piece

GARDENIA
#2 PETAL
Cut 1 white piece

GARDENIA
#1 PETAL
Cut 1 white piece

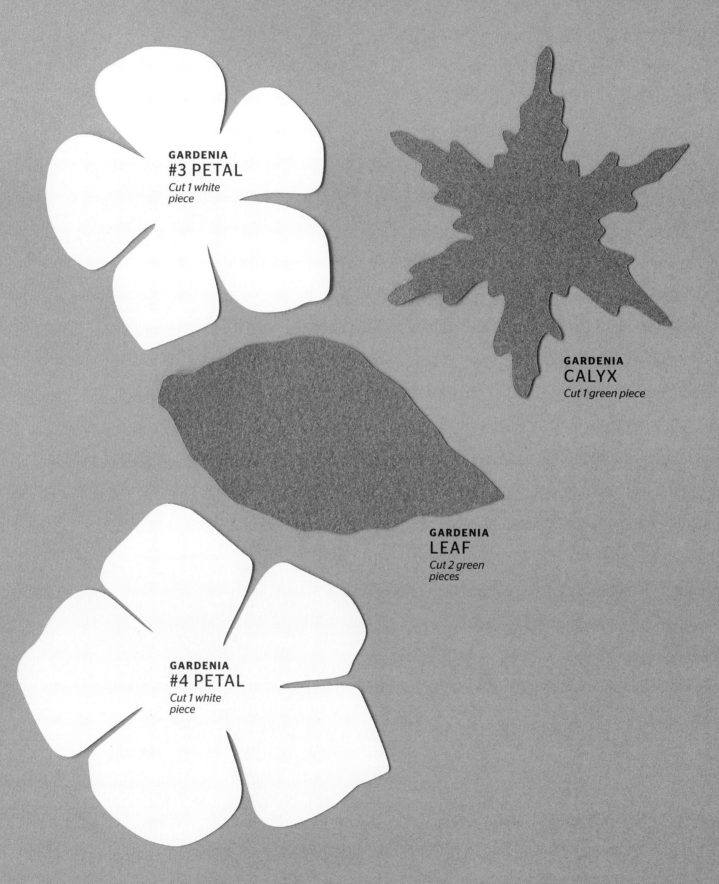

GARDENIA
#3 PETAL
Cut 1 white piece

GARDENIA
CALYX
Cut 1 green piece

GARDENIA
LEAF
Cut 2 green pieces

GARDENIA
#4 PETAL
Cut 1 white piece

PATTERNS

CHRYSANTHEMUM
#2 PETAL
Cut 2 yellow pieces

CHRYSANTHEMUM
LEAF
Cut 2 green pieces

CHRYSANTHEMUM
LOCKING DISK
Cut 2 from card stock

CHRYSANTHEMUM
#1 PETAL
Cut 2 yellow pieces

CHRYSANTHEMUM
CALYX
Cut 1 green piece

CHRYSANTHEMUM
#3 PETAL
Cut 2 yellow pieces

CHRYSANTHEMUM
#4 PETAL
Cut 2 yellow pieces

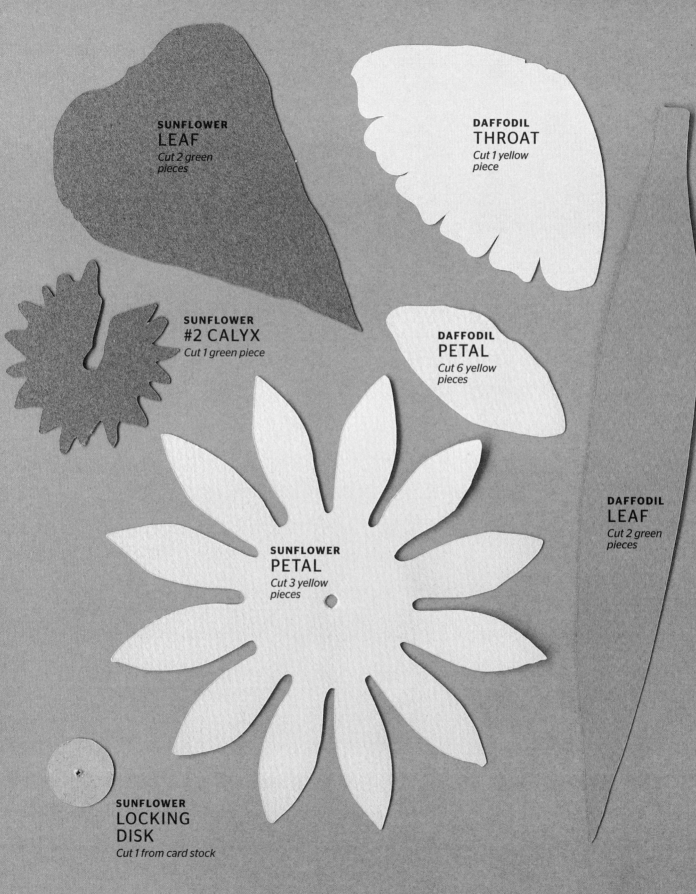

SUNFLOWER
LEAF
Cut 2 green pieces

DAFFODIL
THROAT
Cut 1 yellow piece

SUNFLOWER
#2 CALYX
Cut 1 green piece

DAFFODIL
PETAL
Cut 6 yellow pieces

SUNFLOWER
PETAL
Cut 3 yellow pieces

DAFFODIL
LEAF
Cut 2 green pieces

SUNFLOWER
LOCKING DISK
Cut 1 from card stock

SUNFLOWER
STAMEN
BACK
Cut 1 from card stock

SUNFLOWER
#1 CALYX
Cut 1 brown piece

SUNFLOWER
STAMEN
Cut 1 from brown felt

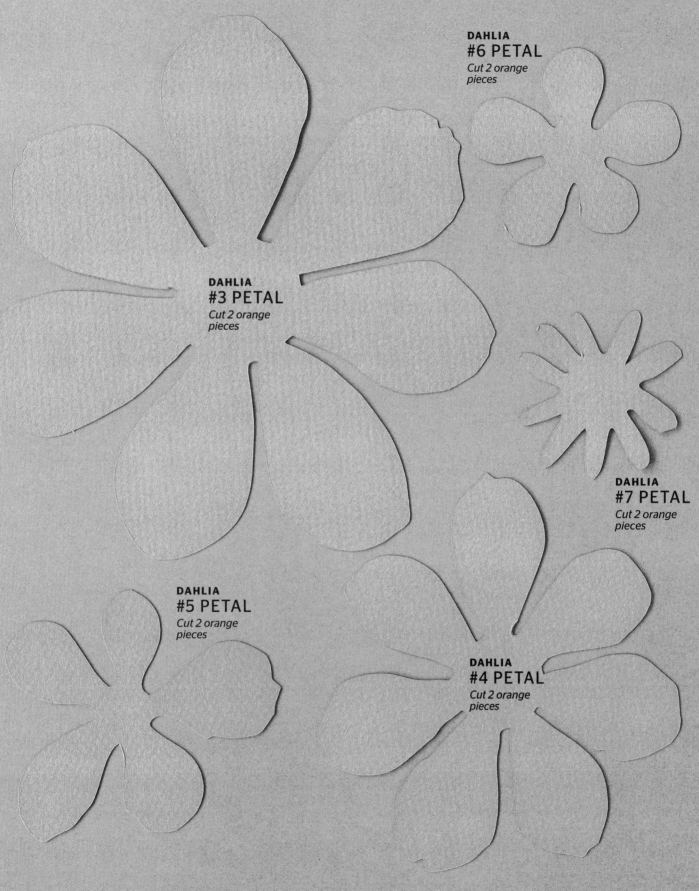

DAHLIA
#6 PETAL
Cut 2 orange pieces

DAHLIA
#3 PETAL
Cut 2 orange pieces

DAHLIA
#7 PETAL
Cut 2 orange pieces

DAHLIA
#5 PETAL
Cut 2 orange pieces

DAHLIA
#4 PETAL
Cut 2 orange pieces

PATTERNS

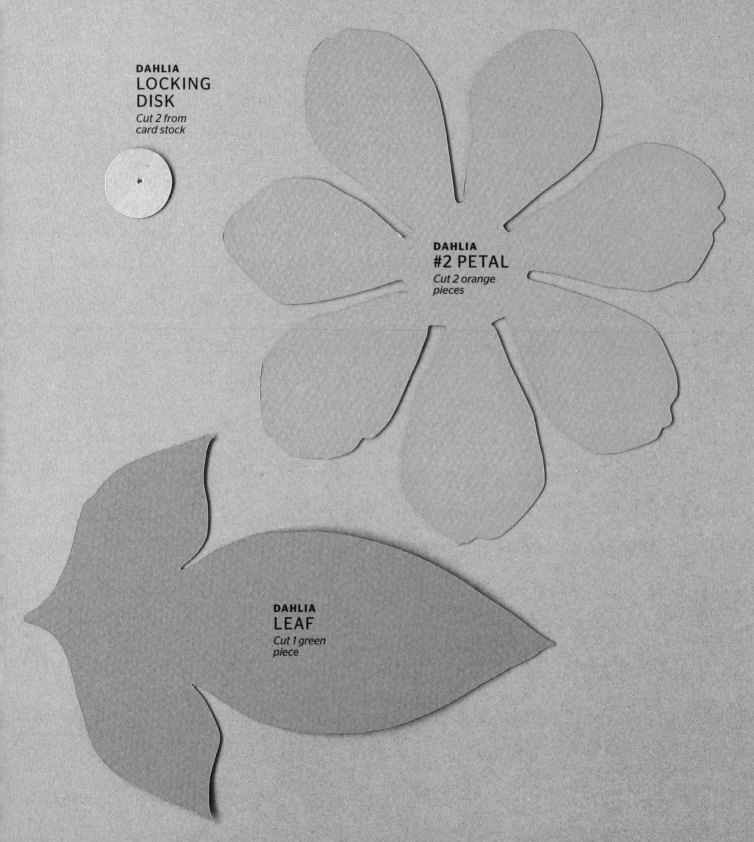

DAHLIA
LOCKING
DISK
*Cut 2 from
card stock*

DAHLIA
#2 PETAL
*Cut 2 orange
pieces*

DAHLIA
LEAF
*Cut 1 green
piece*

DAHLIA
#1 PETAL
Cut 2 orange pieces

DAHLIA
CALYX
Cut 1 green piece

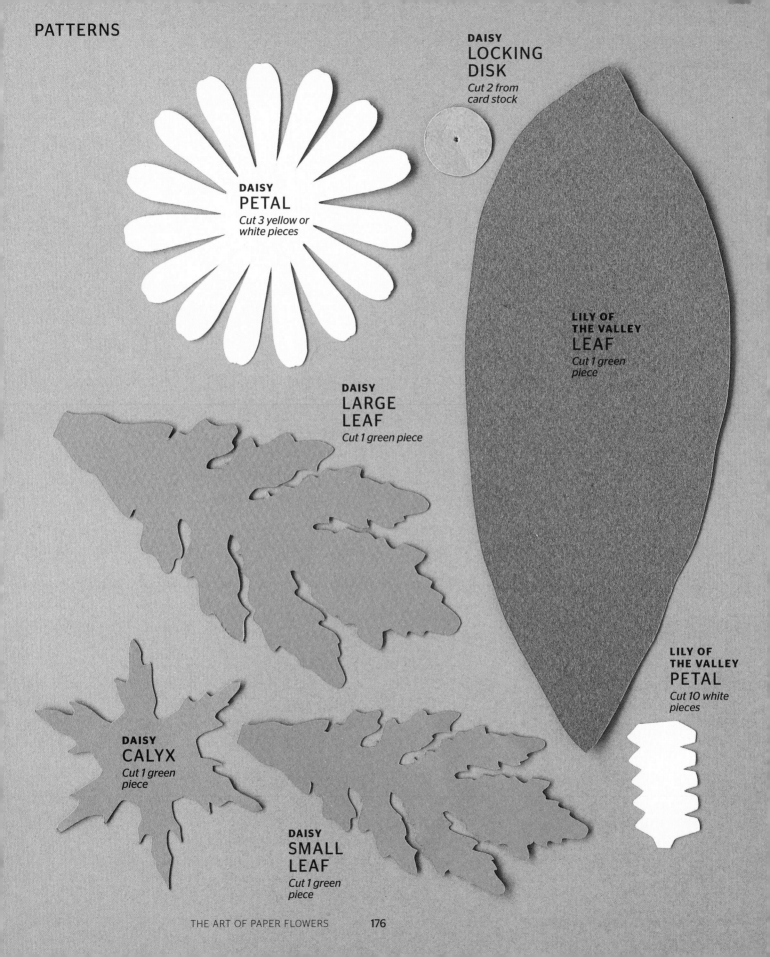

DAISY
PETAL
Cut 3 yellow or white pieces

DAISY
LOCKING DISK
Cut 2 from card stock

LILY OF THE VALLEY
LEAF
Cut 1 green piece

DAISY
LARGE LEAF
Cut 1 green piece

LILY OF THE VALLEY
PETAL
Cut 10 white pieces

DAISY
CALYX
Cut 1 green piece

DAISY
SMALL LEAF
Cut 1 green piece

LILAC
PETAL

Cut 25 purple pieces

LILAC
LEAF

Cut 1 green piece

HYACINTH
LEAF

Cut 5 green pieces

APPLE BLOSSOM
LEAF

Cut 1 green piece

APPLE BLOSSOM
CALYX

Cut 1 green piece

APPLE BLOSSOM
PETAL

Cut 5 pink pieces

WATER LILY
CALYX

Cut 8 green pieces

WATER LILY
SMALL PETAL

Cut 10 white pieces

WATER LILY
LARGE PETAL

Cut 12 white pieces

HYACINTH
PETAL

Cut 40 purple pieces

WATER LILY
LEAF
Cut 3 green pieces

PURPLE ORCHID
LEAF
Cut 2 green pieces

PURPLE ORCHID
THROAT
Cut 1 purple piece

WATER LILY
MEDIUM PETAL
Cut 8 white pieces

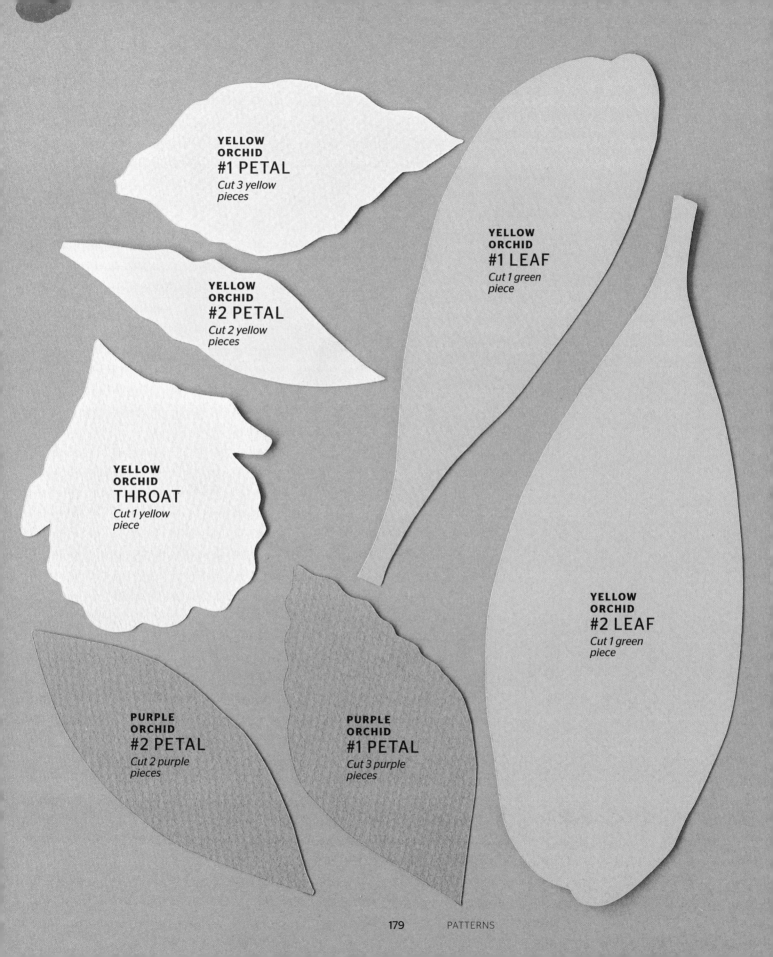

YELLOW ORCHID #1 PETAL

Cut 3 yellow pieces

YELLOW ORCHID #2 PETAL

Cut 2 yellow pieces

YELLOW ORCHID THROAT

Cut 1 yellow piece

YELLOW ORCHID #1 LEAF

Cut 1 green piece

YELLOW ORCHID #2 LEAF

Cut 1 green piece

PURPLE ORCHID #2 PETAL

Cut 2 purple pieces

PURPLE ORCHID #1 PETAL

Cut 3 purple pieces

PATTERNS

PHALAENOPSIS ORCHID
#2 PETAL
Cut 3 purple pieces

PHALAENOPSIS ORCHID
#1 PETAL
Cut 1 purple piece

POINSETTIA
LEAF
Cut 2 green pieces

PHALAENOPSIS ORCHID
LEAF
Cut 2 green pieces

POINSETTIA
#3 PETAL
Cut 3 red pieces

PHALAENOPSIS ORCHID
THROAT
Cut 1 purple piece

POINSETTIA
#1 PETAL
Cut 4 red pieces

POINSETTIA
#2 PETAL
Cut 3 red pieces

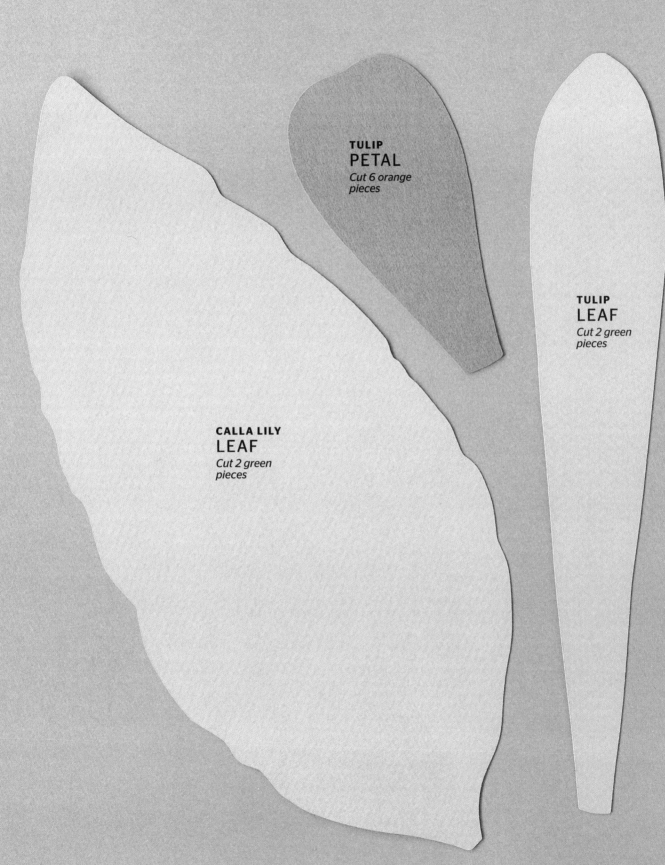

TULIP
PETAL
Cut 6 orange pieces

TULIP
LEAF
Cut 2 green pieces

CALLA LILY
LEAF
Cut 2 green pieces

CALLA LILY
PETAL
Cut 1 white piece

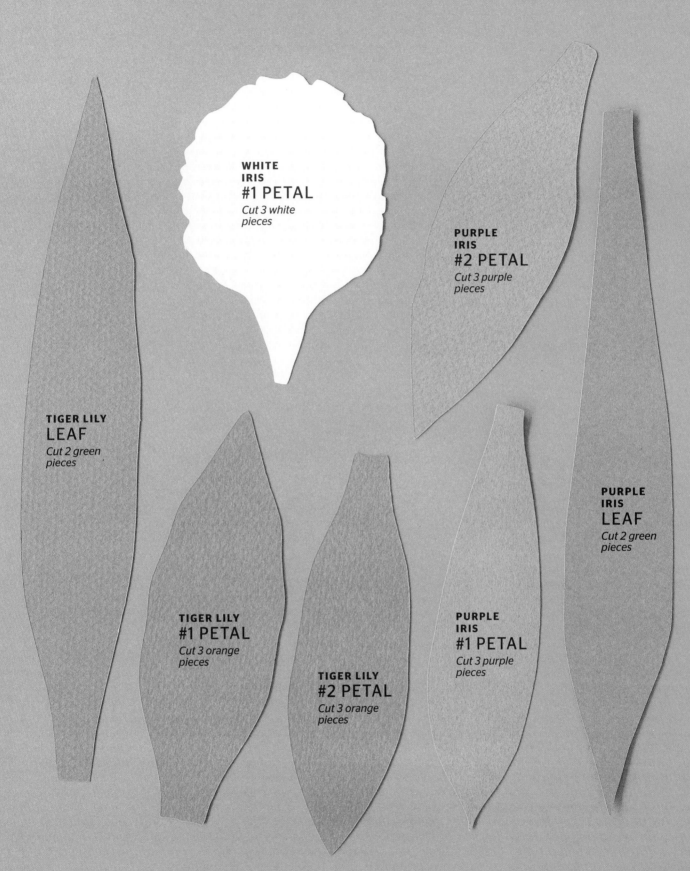

**WHITE
IRIS
#1 PETAL**
*Cut 3 white
pieces*

**PURPLE
IRIS
#2 PETAL**
*Cut 3 purple
pieces*

**TIGER LILY
LEAF**
*Cut 2 green
pieces*

**PURPLE
IRIS
LEAF**
*Cut 2 green
pieces*

**TIGER LILY
#1 PETAL**
*Cut 3 orange
pieces*

**TIGER LILY
#2 PETAL**
*Cut 3 orange
pieces*

**PURPLE
IRIS
#1 PETAL**
*Cut 3 purple
pieces*

PATTERNS

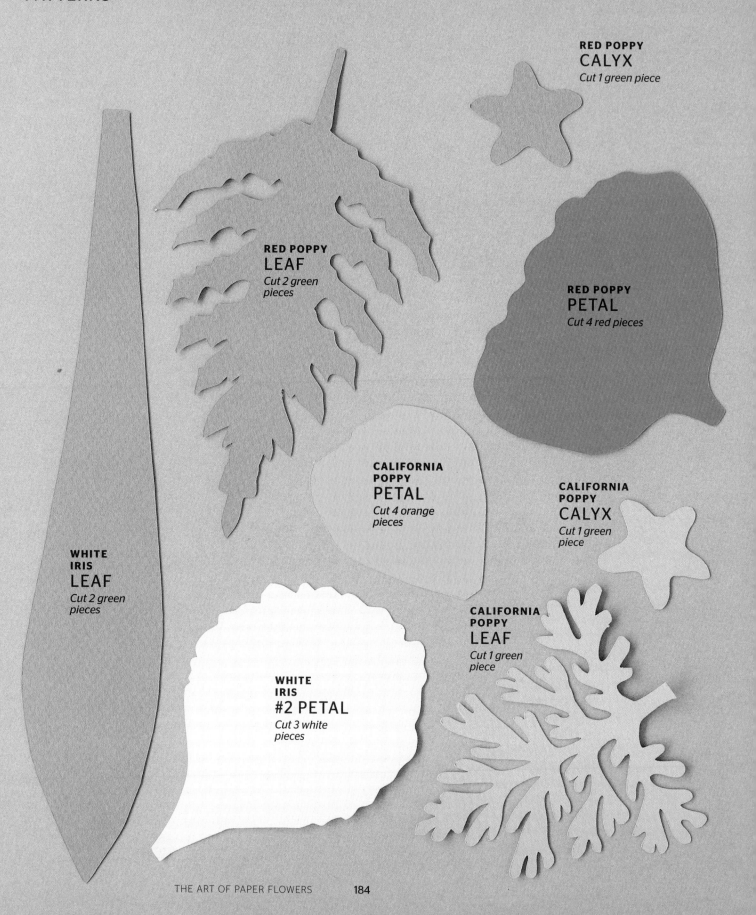

RED POPPY
CALYX
Cut 1 green piece

RED POPPY
LEAF
Cut 2 green pieces

RED POPPY
PETAL
Cut 4 red pieces

CALIFORNIA POPPY
PETAL
Cut 4 orange pieces

CALIFORNIA POPPY
CALYX
Cut 1 green piece

WHITE IRIS
LEAF
Cut 2 green pieces

CALIFORNIA POPPY
LEAF
Cut 1 green piece

WHITE IRIS
#2 PETAL
Cut 3 white pieces

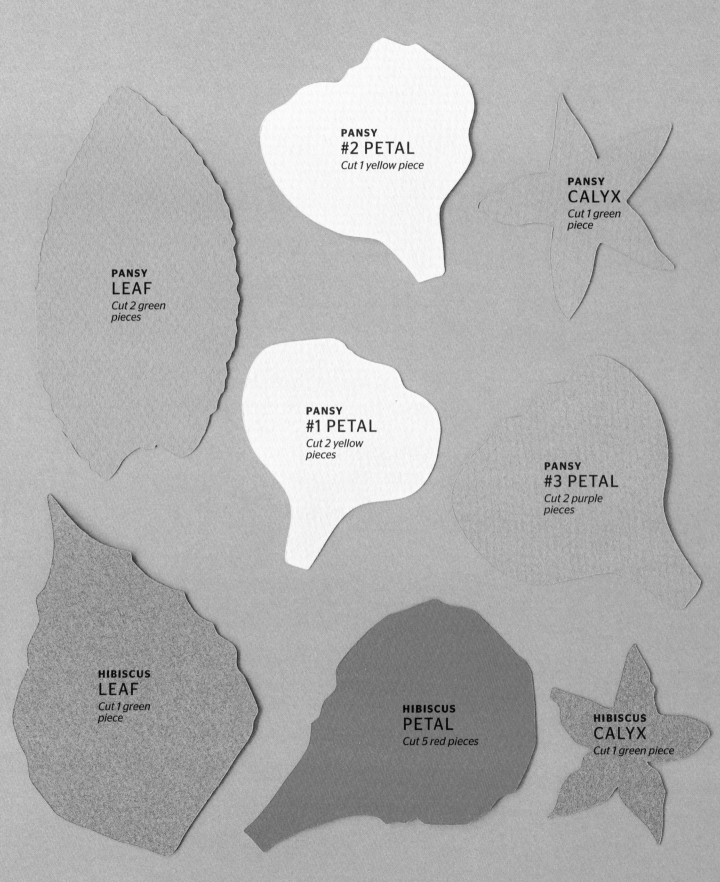

PANSY
#2 PETAL
Cut 1 yellow piece

PANSY
CALYX
Cut 1 green piece

PANSY
LEAF
Cut 2 green pieces

PANSY
#1 PETAL
Cut 2 yellow pieces

PANSY
#3 PETAL
Cut 2 purple pieces

HIBISCUS
LEAF
Cut 1 green piece

HIBISCUS
PETAL
Cut 5 red pieces

HIBISCUS
CALYX
Cut 1 green piece

ANTHURIUM
LEAF
Cut 1 green piece

SWEET PEA
CALYX
Cut 1 green piece

SWEET PEA
#1 PETAL
Cut 1 blue piece

SWEET PEA
#2 PETAL
Cut 1 blue piece

SWEET PEA
LEAF
Cut 1 green piece

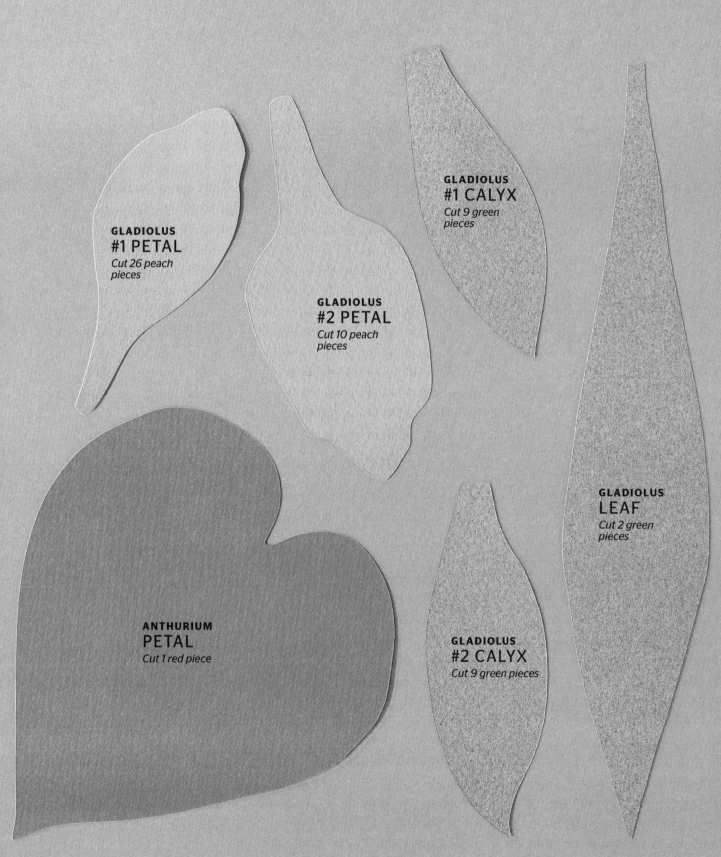

GLADIOLUS
#1 PETAL
Cut 26 peach pieces

GLADIOLUS
#2 PETAL
Cut 10 peach pieces

GLADIOLUS
#1 CALYX
Cut 9 green pieces

GLADIOLUS
LEAF
Cut 2 green pieces

ANTHURIUM
PETAL
Cut 1 red piece

GLADIOLUS
#2 CALYX
Cut 9 green pieces

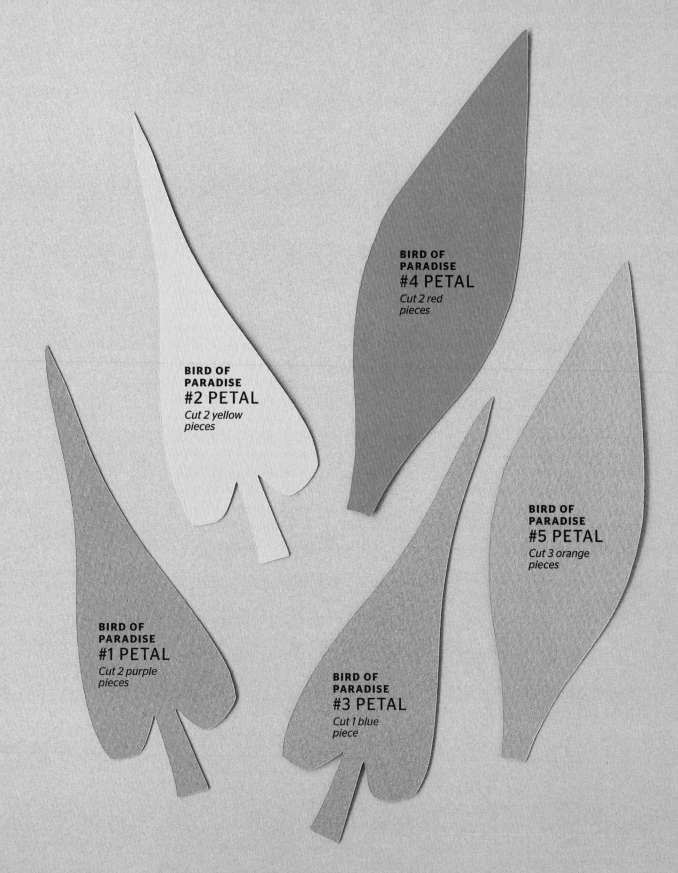

BIRD OF
PARADISE
#4 PETAL
*Cut 2 red
pieces*

BIRD OF
PARADISE
#2 PETAL
*Cut 2 yellow
pieces*

BIRD OF
PARADISE
#5 PETAL
*Cut 3 orange
pieces*

BIRD OF
PARADISE
#1 PETAL
*Cut 2 purple
pieces*

BIRD OF
PARADISE
#3 PETAL
*Cut 1 blue
piece*